Breadmaking Technology

An Introduction to Bread Baking in North America

By
WULF T. DOERRY
Director, Cereal Technology
American Institute of Baking

Published by:

AMERICAN INSTITUTE OF BAKING
Manhattan, Kansas 66502

I

Contents

Chapter Four

Chapter Five

Chapter Six

Chapter Seven

Chapter Eight

Index

Preface

During the 40 plus years that the author has been associated with the baking industry, he has seen and experienced many changes in the product mix offered by this industry, in the baking technology used and, most of all, in the training and qualifications of the supervisory personnel. The emphasis for supervisory training has shifted from long years of "hands on" experience in manufacturing to a more formal training stressing personnel management and which may even include a college education. Product development has moved from the production floor to a baking laboratory staffed by food scientists and baking technologists with very little experience on the production floor. However, these same scientists and technologists are expected to provide the necessary support for production personnel who often have a very good understanding of how to operate the specific production line they are trained on, but have only a limited understanding of the natural forces which determine the quality of the finished product.

Although there is no susbstitute for personal experience in bakery production, the author was encouraged by Dr. James L. Vetter, Vice President-Technical, American Institute of Baking (AIB), to share his vast experience in the baking industry with those who find themselves in bakery production with a need for a better understanding of the breadmaking technologies used on the North American continent. This volume is the first in a series of specialized books on baking technology to be published by AIB.

The need for this book manifested itself in the many technical questions directed to staff at the AIB by bakers and food technologists who have very limited background in baking technology and who have asked for a source of information covered in this book.

The objective of this book is not only to acquaint the reader with the various technologies used for the manufacture of bread on the North American continent, but to also provide basic information on equipment used by the bread baking industry. This book is helpful not only to production management personnel, but especially to anyone who must become familiar with various breadmaking technologies in a very short time span. The author made a special effort to explain complex issues in an easy to read and understand language. Terminology is explained within the text and should not require a special dictionary. This makes this book especially useful to persons for whom English is a second language.

However, this book could never have been written and published without the counsel the author received from AIB personnel and from representatives of allied industries. My special thanks go to Dr. Vetter, who provided the necessary time and encouragement, to Martin Puntney, who took some of the equipment pictures and who put this book into its final form, to Donald Dubois, who helped to edit the manuscript, to Anita Ricklefs for spell-checking the manuscript and putting it into a presentable form, and to Elizabeth Brock for proofreading and checking the text for syntax. The author also thanks all those at AIB and in the allied industries, who checked portions of the manuscript for accuracy and those, who provided pictures of equipment reproduced in this book.

The author also thanks his family for the support and encouragement provided for this change in his career.

As mentioned earlier, this treatise is only the first in a series of books covering various baking technologies. Some of the future books will contain a variety of formulations which have been developed and/or test-baked at AIB and may be especially useful to baking technologists active in product development. Although future books will be written in a similar style, repitition of presented material will be minimal and limited to some very essential information.

Manhattan, Kansas
April 1995

Evolution of Breadmaking

Bread evolved gradually. Its history is laced with assumptions and speculation about what may have happened, but much is based on logic and preserved customs.

Before the development of suitable ovens during the Egyptian dynasties, the first "bread products" were most likely flat breads. These types of bread are still produced and eaten in many parts of the world. The idea of *baking* probably came from an accident: someone may have spilled grain mush or gruel onto a hot stone or into a fire and discovered the "baked" product was still edible. Further experimentation may have revealed that gruel baked on a hot rock not only tasted good but was also easier to store and to transport. Moreover, this type of flat bread could provide a base for other foods, or it could be eaten by itself. The flat breads of the Middle East, the pizza in Italy, the chapati of India, and the tortilla in Mexico all could have originated in such an accident.

There is probably a good reason why flat breads are not a staple food in the colder regions of the world. Here one may speculate that it must have been very difficult and inefficient during the cold season to heat a stone over a fire for baking the gruel. Also, the colder regions lagged behind in agricultural development. The climate there was not as favorable for growing the crops found in the Medi-

Early breadmaking techniques are depicted in this relief from ancient Egypt.

terranean region which was the cradle for many early civilizations. By the time the Germanic people in central and northern Europe established a flourishing agriculture based on faster growing rye, they had already been exposed to spontaneous fermentation of cereal doughs and to the more energy efficient ovens used by the Romans who occupied part of their territory. These ovens made it possible to bake larger pieces and quantities of dough for a longer period of time and with a reasonable amount of fuel.

Rye flours posed special problems, however. As is well known by traditional rye bread bakers, doughs made from 100% rye flour must be "sour." If not, the high level of amylase enzymes in the rye flour will cause the crumb in the baked product to collapse during baking and to separate from the crust. This required acidity, or "sourness," is produced by yeast and/or bacteria during fermentation. The acidic environment also provides the optimum conditions for the phytase enzymes in the dough to break down phytic acid, which is concentrated in wheat and rye immediately below the bran layer of the grain. Phytic acid combines with multivalent metallic ions (Fretzdorff and Bruemmer 1992), such as calcium, iron, copper, and zinc, and thus interferes with the absorption of these minerals in the digestive tract. Thus, most of the iron and calcium in whole wheat and rye meal cannot be utilized by human beings unless the phytic acid is broken down by the enzyme phytase.

Since the breakdown of phytic acid occurs to a greater extent in acidified doughs, people consuming large amounts of whole grain benefit significantly from allowing their doughs to ferment naturally to a high acid content. As reported by Fretzdorff and Bruemmer (1992), the phytase is most active in doughs with a pH of about 4.5. Also, a finer grind of the flour facilitates the enzymatic breakdown of the phytic acid in the grain.

Even though the agricultural people in the moderate and cooler climates of Europe were most likely not aware of the intrinsic nutritional value of long fermentation periods, it is probably no coincidence that most northern agricultural civilizations developed a technology for fermenting doughs. Much of their diet depended on grains easily grown and stored in these northern regions. The failure to ferment these grains would have deprived them of some very important minerals. Fermented doughs also produce more flavorful breads with better keeping quality. In addition, the leavening action also produces an improved crumb texture. Both these facts may have benefitted these early consumers more than commonly recognized.

The necessity to "bake" bread in ovens, rather than quickly on a hot stone, led to the preparation of larger *doughs,* or batches, which better retained the heat generated during spontaneous fermentation. Initially, new batches of dough were most likely inoculated by remnants of previous batches left in the container used for preparing the dough. In more recent times bakers usually saved a chunk of the last dough made that day as a *starter* for new doughs to be made in the near future. The exchange of good *sour dough starters* between families and friends was a common practice until commercial yeasts became widely available during the late 1800s.

Although commercial bakeries have existed for more than 2000 years, prior to this century the quality of their products was variable. The absence of a uniform quality standard invited some bakers to cheat on the public. Laws that inflicted severe punishment on those who violated the early consumer protection laws countered this trend. The term *baker's dozen* (13 units instead of 12 units per dozen) originated in England during the medieval era when bakers were afraid of being accused of giving their customers less than a full count.

The overall quality of bread offered to the general public started to improve when commercial yeast became available and bakers started to better understand the fermentation process. They learned how to control time and temperature in order to obtain the best results. Since the beginning of the 20th century, more and more specialty ingredients (bread improvers) became available and improvements in equipment design made it possible to produce large quantities of high quality bread with a very limited labor force. The complete control over the fermentation process was a prerequisite for this achievement.

Available bread-making technology was very limited until after World War II, but is quite diversified today. Until the early 1970s, technical service personnel from mills and yeast companies had easy access to most bakeries in the United States. This resulted, even though not officially, in the standardization of the manufacturing process for white pan bread. But this has changed! Bakers have become very secretive and no longer freely share their experiences. Bakers now use a variety of mixers and preferment systems. Also, the baking ingredient industry has responded to the special needs of individual bakeries for dough strengthening and for extending the shelf-life of their finished product with a large assortment of dough conditioners and crumb softeners. All this has created such a diversity in formulations and technology, that there are now hardly two bakeries producing bakery foods in the same way.

Straight Dough Technology

The dough-making process inherited from the Egyptians is now called the *straight dough method*. This term implies that all ingredients for a bread dough are added *straight* to the mixer, i.e., at one time. This method does not utilize a flour preferment. In some cases salt is added after the dough is partially mixed because it tends to interfere with the gluten development in the dough.

Except for the use of commercial yeast and optional dough ingredients, the technology used for straight doughs today does not differ very much from that used one hundred or one thousand years ago. The wheat is now milled into refined and treated flour instead of being ground into whole meal, the water is filtered and treated, and the doughs are mixed with a mechanical mixer instead of kneaded by hand. But, in order to obtain the best quality bread by this method, the dough must still be properly conditioned either through fermentation or with "maturing" agents, such as oxidants.

The straight dough method can be used for the production of all types of bread, ranging from French bread to white pan bread and rye breads. Bakers use two slightly different straight dough methods. The traditional method utilizes a *bulk fermentation* period, during which the dough is "conditioned" by fermentation, i.e., production of fermentation acids. When the baker uses this procedure, the dough is mixed to full development at 78-81° Fahrenheit (F) or 25.5-27° Celsius (C). Depending on the formulation and the amount of yeast added, straight doughs are fermented in a "warm" place (about 82-84°F or 28-29°C) for 1.5-3 hours. The baker will usually "punch" (knock down) the dough at least once after it expands to a point of maximum volume. This practice originated a long time ago when doughs were mixed by hand and yeast was scarce and expensive. The punching process added further gluten development to the dough. At the same time the baker would "fold" the dough. This process added oxygen to the dough which stimulated the yeast to propagate. This was very important at a time when bakers used very low yeast levels or depended on the wild yeast in their "starters."

A new type of straight dough became popular during the late 1960s. It was called the *no-time straight dough* method. This type of dough technology is the direct consequence of changing times: the advent of high-speed mechanical mixing, cheaper yeast, availability of oxidizing agents for *chemical dough development*, and increasing labor cost, i.e., a good potential for time savings. Although no-time doughs are prepared with any kind of bread mixer, they were originally promoted primarily with the use of high-speed mixers such as the Chorleywood method for the Tweedy mixer.

No-time doughs are mixed to the slightly warmer temperature of 82-84°F (28-29°C) and receive no significant bulk fermentation. They are generally transferred to the dough divider within 10 to 20 minutes after mixing. All further processing is the same as for other doughs. Since no-time doughs are not subjected to bulk fermentation, they do not require "degassing" prior to dividing. These doughs generally process slightly better through all make-up equipment than regular straight doughs. However, since the no-time doughs are not "conditioned" by the fermentation process, this must be done through the addition of extra "maturing" (oxidizing) agents, such as 60-120 parts of ascorbic acid per million parts (ppm) of flour. Bakery ingredient suppliers offer a large selection of ingredients specifically formulated for no-time doughs. Most of these also contain L-cysteine to reduce the time it takes to develop the gluten, i.e., to mix the dough in less time.

Although shortening the dough processing time by eliminating the bulk fermentation period is a significant advantage to the baker, the lack of fermentation has an adverse effect on the flavor and shelf-life of the baked product. While the lack of flavor is generally not much of a problem when the bread is very fresh, it is very noticeable when the no-time dough product is compared side by side with properly fermented bread, particularly after the product has staled (aged) slightly. The shelf-life of the bakery food is also adversely affected by the lack of "conditioning" through fermentation. The crumb formed during baking from a well fermented dough tends to become firm at a slower rate than the crumb from a similar dough that has not been fermented in bulk. However, by using the proper dough oxidants (ascorbic acid and/or azodicarbonamide), dough conditioner (monocalcium phosphate and/or calcium sulfate), and perhaps enzymes, bread of a good volume and with a good crumb texture can be produced from no-time doughs.

Sponge Dough Technology

The word *sponge* is a term having a special meaning for the baker and is not part of the definition given in a dictionary for the English language. The baker applies the term "sponge" to a preferment made from flour, water, yeast, and some minor additives which help to condition or to strengthen the flour in the dough. When this preferment is fully fermented and conditioned, its appearance somewhat resembles that of an ordinary sponge used for cleaning.

There is no rule prescribing the amount of total flour in the formula which should be prefermented. Although the percent of flour in the preferment could range from 10-100%, the baking industry in the United States usually limits this to a range of 40-80% of the total flour. As a general rule, the less "floor time" (bulk fermentation period after mixing) is given to the dough, the greater the percentage of the flour in the "sponge." Bakers who give their doughs only 5-10 minutes floor time preferment 80% of the total flour in the sponge. On the other hand, bakers using only 60% of the flour in the sponge get best results when they give their freshly mixed doughs 30-45 minutes floor time, depending on the dough temperature. Bakers usually shorten the floor time slightly for doughs with a temperature above 80°F (27°C) or lengthen it for doughs cooler than desired.

The baking industry uses two types of sponges. *Plastic sponges* are generally used when more than 55% of the total flour is prefermented. Plastic sponges receive minimal mixing, just enough for the flour to absorb the water and to make sure that the yeast and other ingredients are properly distributed in the sponge. The water absorption of plastic sponges is generally limited to a range of 58-62% of the flour in the sponge. This amount of water gives the sponge a relatively dry and firm, or "plastic" consistency, in the unfermented stage. As fermentation proceeds, the preferment is expanded by fermentation gases and assumes a "spongy" appearance. Some bakers also call this type of sponge a *solid sponge*, to differentiate it from the second type, the *liquid sponge*.

Liquid sponges contain at least as much water as flour. The ratio of water to flour can be as high as 1.25:1.00, but is generally between 1.05 and 1.15:1.00. The limiting factor is the heat exchanger which must reduce the temperature of the fully fermented liquid sponge to slow down further yeast activity. While very "stiff" sponges are difficult to pump through plate heat exchangers, very fluid sponges may cause a problem with gluten separating from the slurry and clogging the heat exchanger plates. Although some bakers use higher or lower amounts of flour in their liquid sponges, most of them preferment about 30-50% of the total flour in the formula.

Bakers tend to add all the yeast to the sponge. In liquid sponges, the yeast level is usually about 0.5% flour basis (f.b., explained in the next chapter), higher than the 2-2.5% (f.b.) compressed or crumbled yeast normally added to plastic sponges. Depending on ambient conditions prevailing in the area where the fermentation is to take place, plastic sponges are generally "set" at (mixed to) a temperature of 72-77°F (22-25°C). During the cold season the baker may prefer the warmer temperature, but during the summer, when bakeries tend to be warmer, cooler temperatures are usually chosen.

The temperature of liquid preferments can be controlled more easily, and these sponges are usually "set" at slightly higher temperatures than plastic sponges. Liquid sponges formulated with less than 30% of the total flour may be started at a temperature as high as 82-84°F (28-29°C), in order to keep their total fermentation time as short as possible. Fermentation reactions are very sensitive to temperature and a difference of a few degrees can have a big effect on the time it takes for the sponge to ferment properly. However, warmer preferments tend to produce off-flavors more readily than cooler sponges, and a good control over the temperature maintained in the fermentation tanks is essential for the manufacture of high-quality bread products.

While plastic sponges are allowed to retain the heat developed during fermentation of sugars in the dough, liquid sponges are often fermented at a specified temperature in a jacketed stainless steel tank. Sweep-wall agitation keeps the sponge at a constant temperature through heat transfer to the refrigerated cooling jacket (double wall with cavity between walls filled with a refrigerated or heated fluid for heat exchange). Therefore, liquid sponges are ideal for fully automated bakeries, which require complete control over their preferments.

Depending on the temperature and on the yeast level in the preferment, plastic sponges are usually fermented for three to six hours. Most bakeries, however, ferment plastic sponges for 3.5-4.5 hours. During this time, the temperature of the sponge generally rises between 7-10°F (4-5.5°C). Longer fermentation times are usually needed with low levels of yeast in the sponge. To keep the proof time at about 60 minutes, the doughs made from slowly fermented sponges are often "spiked" (boosted) at the remix stage with an additional small amount of yeast. The same is sometimes necessary for doughs made from liquid sponges.

Because liquid ferments are normally fermented at higher temperatures than plastic sponges, their fermentation time is usually slightly shorter. As a general rule, the less flour in the liquid ferment, the shorter the fermentation time and the warmer the setting (initial) temperature for the sponge. Also, when the flour in the preferment is less than 30% of the total flour in the final dough, a small amount of sugar (about one percent of the total flour weight) is usually added to the sponge to provide sufficient fermentable solids. Higher levels of sugar tend to produce more organic acids and lower the pH of the preferment more rapidly; but when the pH in the ferment becomes very low, the high acidity starts to have an adverse effect on the crumb structure of the baked product. This potential problem does not exist in liquid sponges prepared with 40% or more of the total flour, because the flour not only provides sufficient sugar for the fermentation, but it also has a very good buffering effect on the pH of the preferment.

The fermentation time for liquid sponges varies from about 1.5 hours for a very low flour content to about 3 hours when 50% or more of the flour is prefermented. Liquid sponges are fermented and stored in stainless steel tanks, which require significantly less floor-space than the equipment used for plastic sponges. With the development of new metering devices, liquid sponges of all densities can now be transferred quickly and accurately to mixers.

Water Brews

Water brews were very popular during the 1970s. But during the 1980s, bakers gradually replaced these brews with liquid sponges or they returned to using plastic sponges, provided the plant did not suffer from a severe lack of space. Although product manufactured from water brews has a very good eye appeal, many bakers and consumers agree that it lacks a good flavor and shelf-life. Today, very few bakers still use the water brew method for manufacturing their breads.

Water brews contain very little (less than 10% of the total flour in the dough) or no flour. All the fermentable solids in the brew are added as sugar, primarily as high-fructose corn syrup. Since these water brews contain no significant amount of flour, a chemical buffer must be added to prevent the pH of the brew from dropping to such a low level that it inhibits the yeast. This chemical buffer generally consists of a blend of calcium carbonate, ammonium sulfate, and calcium sulfate. Some salt and flour or starch are often added to dilute the mix for more accurate scaling. The baker usually formulates the water brew with about two-thirds of the total dough water (40-45% of the flour weight in the formula), about 2% (f.b.) sugar solids, all the yeast (about 3% f.b.), 0.5% f.b. salt, and 0.2% f.b. brew buffer. The mix is allowed to ferment for about 1.5-2 hours at 82 to 84°F (28 to 29°C), or until there is no further drop in the pH of the brew.

Since the added sugar is the only source of fermentables for the yeast, the amount of sugar in the brew has a significant effect on the final pH and on the total acid content in the brew. However, most of the acid in the brew is carbonic acid, which forms when carbon dioxide dissolves in water. Because the solubility of carbon dioxide is inversely related to the temperature, higher fermentation temperatures for water brews generally result in lower amounts of acid retained by the brew. Also, except for some sourness, carbonic acid contributes very little to the overall flavor of bread. This may have been an important factor in the decision of some bakers to abandon this bread-making technology in favor of flour preferments.

Sours

The original and natural method for leavening bread came from microorganisms introduced into the dough mass by accidental contamination, either with contaminated utensils, with ingredients, or as airborne spores. Types of bacteria and wild yeasts present and propagating in a sour dough are generally more influenced by the conditions they find in the medium than by choice of the baker. Different organisms favor different media. Some organisms may also produce different fermentation products as the conditions in the medium change, e.g., temperature and availability of nutrients.

Microorganisms in sour doughs consist of two different types: bacteria and yeast. Although there are exceptions, the end-products of bacterial fermentation are primarily organic acids. Yeasts produce mainly alcohol and carbon dioxide. While the carbon dioxide provides the "leavening" (expansion of gas cells) for doughs, the organic acids help to condition the protein in the dough and, in the case of rye doughs, to suppress excessive amylolytic enzyme activity. Although carbon dioxide contributes to the acidity of the product by forming carbonic acid, it adds very little flavor to the bread beyond the sour taste. The flavor comes from the various organic acids produced by bacteria, which may or may not react with each other, and with the alcohol from yeast fermentation to form flavorful esters during the baking process.

The most desirable organic acids are produced by heterofermentative (producing a variety of fermentation products) lactic acid bacteria. Although these organisms produce primarily lactic acid, they also synthesize, or produce, other organic acids. The kind of acid produced depends on the type and temperature of the material fermented, which is called the substrate. Generally, lower fermentation temperatures favor the formation of desirable organic acids, such as acetic, citric, lactic, fumaric, malic, and others. Higher fermentation temperatures, however, seem to favor the formation of butyric and slightly longer chain fatty acids, which tend to result in undesirable flavors.

Bakers rely on a variety of methods for making sour doughs. The easiest way is to obtain a *sour dough starter* from another source. During the past 30 years, many bakers were interested in reproducing San Francisco sour dough bread. But, despite great effort and expense, only a few bakers succeeded in producing a satisfactory product. Most of them learned very quickly that the sour dough starter they obtained in San Francisco could not be frozen. Subsequent research revealed that the San Francisco sour dough contained a specific lactic acid bacterium (*L. sanfrancisco*) and a unique yeast strain, which thrives under high acid (low pH) conditions and is unable to ferment maltose. This yeast does not survive freezing.

It is easy to contaminate a starter with unwanted microbes which suppress the organisms producing the desirable fermentation products. Consequently, only a few bakers finally managed to produce an acceptable sour dough bread for sale. However, the difficulty of starting and maintaining a sour dough culture provided an opportunity for commercial laboratories to develop and offer to the baking industry an assortment of sour dough cultures, most of them sold in the frozen state. These cultures generally resulted in mildly sour bread of good appearance, but with an off-flavor. Most of these cultures disappeared again from the market as quickly as they appeared. Although still available, sour dough cultures are today more a novelty than a new viable technology. A good reason for this is not only that most sour dough bread has an off-flavor, but also that long proof times at slightly lower than normal temperatures make it difficult for bakers to schedule this type of bread as part of regular production.

To overcome all these difficulties, many bakers who have a market for bread with a mild sour taste have taken advantage of readily available ingredients, which not only add acidity to the dough, but also contribute a good and pleasantly sour flavor. These ingredients are generally offered under the category of *light sour* or *rye sour.* They are usually manufactured from cultured doughs fermented under strictly controlled conditions. After the fermentation process is complete, the doughs are dried and ground to a flour. Since the baker uses these dry sours with regular yeast for leavening, as much of the light or rye sour can be added to doughs as deemed necessary to obtain the desired taste. Enough yeast is also added to control the product's proof time for proper scheduling.

In addition to the two groups of dry sours, there are also flavor concentrates available. These concentrates supplement and intensify the flavor of natural and dry sours with a blend of organic and inorganic acids. Lactic, acetic, and phosphoric acid, as well as calcium salts of phosphoric acid are common ingredients in such flavor concentrates. Bakers tend to use these concentrates more in rye doughs than in white bread.

There is hardly a retail baker in this country who has not attempted to prepare a starter for sour bread. This effort is encouraged by a large number of recipes for starting a spontaneous sour ferment. These recipes advise the use of a wide variety of starting materials, many of which have no obvious quality or property to justify their use. Bakers have used raw onions, potatoes, canned pineapple, regular baker's yeast, and many vegetable sources to inoculate their starter doughs. None of these "starters" can be associated with the presence of high levels of lactic acid bacteria. Also, few bakers ever attempted to perpetuate any of these sours so that they could be used on a continuous basis. It is easily possible that most of the organisms found in starters initiated by bakers were introduced either accidentally or with another ingredient, such as yeast.

A simple way to build up a sour dough starter was suggested by Ziemke and Sanders (1988):

Sour Dough Starter

100 lb.	High Gluten Flour
50 lb.	Water
25 lb.	Starter (cultured sourdough)

The *starter culture* is either purchased from a commercial supplier or derived from an existing sour dough produced at the bakery. These starter cultures contribute viable bacteria and yeast cells for the fermentation of the sour dough.

The starter culture is used for the preparation of the *sour dough starter*. The starter provides a good environment for the bacteria and yeast cells in the starter culture to multiply. It is set at about 77°F (25°C) and allowed to remain at this temperature for about two hours. After this rest time, the sour dough starter is held for ten hours at a temperature of 39-41°F (4-5°C). This colder temperature suppresses yeast activity and promotes the formation of desirable fermentation acids.

The sour dough starter is usually used at a level of 18-24% of the total flour in the sour dough formula. However, some bakers have also reported higher and lower usage levels. The reason for these variances may be that the starter is either not acidic enough for the desired results, or the baker likes to impart only a very mild sour taste to his bread.

Most *spontaneous sours* do not contain a sufficient number of yeast cells with a good tolerance to a low pH (below 4.8) to generate a sufficient quantity of carbon dioxide for leavening the dough prior to baking. For this reason, a small amount of baker's yeast is usually added to sour doughs. The amount of yeast added usually ranges from 0.125-1.0% of the total weight of flour in the bread formula. Higher levels of baker's yeast will accelerate the "proofing" (rising) process for the sour dough, but may also suppress the acid producing bacteria, which could result in reduced sourness and flavor. A sour dough prepared with more than 0.1% (f.b.) yeast should never be used to start a new sour dough, since the extra yeast will gradually suppress the microorganisms introduced with the original sour dough culture. For this reason, it is always best to retain a small amount of the last sour dough starter as a sour dough culture for inoculating a new starter. This process is known as *perpetuating the sour*.

References

Fretzdorff, B., and Bruemmer, J.M. 1992. Reduction of Phytic Acid During Breadmaking of Whole-Meal Bread. *Cereal Chemistry* Vol. 69, No. 3, 269.

Ziemke, W. H., and Sanders, Scott, Ph.D. 1988. Sourdough Bread, *Technical Bulletin, American Institute of Baking,* Vol. X, No. 10, 1.

CHAPTER

TWO

Baker's Percent

Baker's percent is a unique concept for formulating products and comparing formulations of different doughs and batters. Baker's percent relates the quantities of all ingredients to the total amount of flour or some other major ingredient in the formula. This is equivalent to saying that to every 100 pound (lb.) bag of flour, the baker adds 60 lb. (60%) water and 2 lb. (2%) salt. In order to indicate that the percentages relate to the total flour weight in the formula, the baker often identifies this relationship as "flour basis" (f.b.). Thus the 60 lb. water added per 100 lb. bag of flour in the mixing bowl is expressed as 60% (f.b.).

Sometimes, this relationship to flour is also described as "based on the total weight of flour in the formula equals 100%." If the formula calls for 72 lb. flour and 1.44 lb. (1 lb., 7 ounces) salt, then the percentage of salt is:

$$(1.44 \text{ lb} \div 72 \text{ lb}) \times 100\% \text{ (f.b.)} = 2\% \text{ (f.b.)}$$

The advantage of using "baker's percent" lies in the fact that a change in the amount of any ingredient, except in the base (flour), will affect only the percentage of this individual ingredient. The percentages of all other ingredients will remain constant. Also, since the amounts of all ingredients are expressed relative to the total amount of flour in the formula, it is easy to compare different formulations.

Even though the majority of bakers now use "baker's percent," formulations based on one gallon of water can still be found. Many formulations were once written as one or two gallon doughs. Here, the baker added sufficient flour to the specified amount of water to form a dough of his liking. All other ingredients remained constant. This method was generally used before bakers had scales to weigh their ingredients. It was based on volume measurements, similar to the methods still used by many home bakers.

Another measure for determining a batch size which is no longer commonly used is the *barrel of flour* (bbl), which equates to 196 lb. flour. Although few formulas utilized this weight measure for flour, the volume measure of one barrel (31.5 gallons) was at one time widely used for rating the capacity of mechanical mixers, such as a "2 bbl mixer." Bread dough mixers, however, are now rated according to the total amount of dough they are capable of mixing at one time. Only the size of vertical mixers is still rated according to the liquid volume capacity of the mixing bowl, e.g., "80 quart mixer."

CHAPTER
THREE

Bakery Equipment

Dough Mixers

Even though hand-mixing bread doughs is still practiced today in some underdeveloped parts of the world, it has always been considered very hard and time-consuming work. The first mechanical dough mixers appeared in Europe at the end of the 18th century. They were driven by gears and powered by human labor. The first mechanical dough mixer developed in the United States was patented in 1865. The main shaft was turned with a crank. The basic concept of this mixer was a solid vertical wheel which kneaded the dough between its sides and the wall of the wooden mixing bowl. It had little resemblance to present-day electrically powered horizontal mixers.

Bread doughs are now mixed with a variety of mechanical mixers with capacities ranging from a few pounds up to 3,000 lbs. of dough per batch. Various types of continuous dough mixers, too, are in use. All mixers are designed to develop the "gluten" from the protein in the wheat flour. All mixers do this by kneading the dough rapidly. This involves repeated compressing (kneading) and stretching of the elastic dough. Since different countries have wheats of differing bread-making quality, many have also developed different mechanical dough mixing systems.

A Peerless high speed tilt bowl horizontal mixer. (Photo courtesy of Peerless Machinery Corp.)

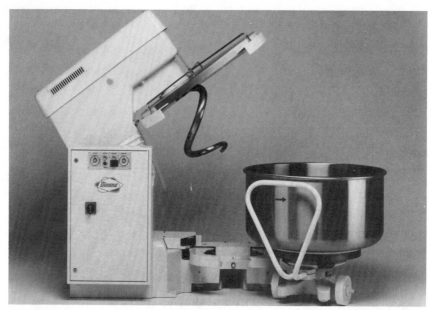

A Benier spiral mixer. (Photo courtesy of Benier USA, Inc.)

While bakers in North America prefer two-speed *horizontal dough mixers* for their relatively strong bread flours, the majority of bakers in Europe use *spiral mixers* to mix their slightly weaker bread flours. In some parts of the world, such as Kenya, even two-speed *double-arm mixers* (Artofex) are used to mix bread doughs. From England comes the *Tweedy mixer*, which mixes doughs to a total energy input level. The texture of the bread from this mixer is controlled by a vacuum in the bowl during mixing. Also from England comes the *BiPlex high-speed mixer*, which uses two different mixing modes to develop the gluten structure in the dough. The *Stephan mixer* from Germany, too, uses a very high-speed dough mixing system.

The state of today's technology makes it possible for practically all mixers to be quickly and automatically "charged" (loaded) with ingredients. Even though the high-speed mixers mix only relatively small doughs at one time, their per hour mixing capacity is quite impressive. The combi-

A Stephan high speed mixer.

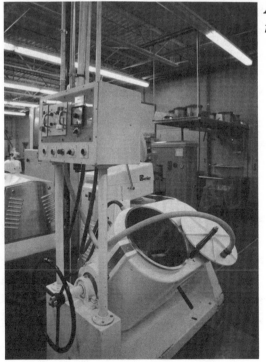

A Tweedy high speed mixer.

nation of fast mixing and complete automation for loading and unloading the mixers makes it possible to produce as many as eight doughs per hour. However, it has been found that flours from the United States require slightly more energy to mix than the average European flour for which most high-speed mixers were developed. Since the European high-speed mixers are generally not designed to cool doughs during mixing, doughs prepared from North American flour tend to pick up more heat energy and thus may be warmer than desired by the baker.

Another reason bakeries in the United States have responded so slowly to the European technology of high-speed mixing is that the automation of these mixers generally does not consider the use of preferments. Even though it would be impractical to set and to process a large number of warm plastic sponges for high-speed mixing, liquid flour preferments can easily be cooled before they are metered and rapidly added to the mixer. A cooled preferment could also help to offset some of the problems caused by the lack of a cooling jacket on high-speed mixers. As it appears now, most bakers in the United States are quite reluctant to use new equipment technology if this also requires significant changes in dough making and processing technology.

In recent years, another type of dough mixer has appeared on the market. This mixer is a single screw or twin screw extruder which mixes doughs continuously. All ingredients are continuously and proportionally introduced into the mixing chamber which has double walls for efficient heating and cooling. The mixing elements on the screw(s) can be changed to meet specific blending or mixing requirements. The extruded dough can then either be subjected to a bulk fermentation period, or it can be divided immediately into individual dough pieces for further processing into loaves or buns. This equipment is easy to

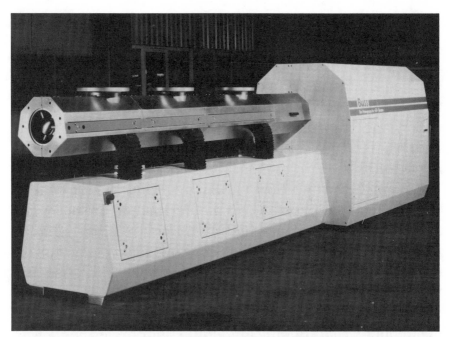

A kneading extruder. (Photo courtesy of Buss America)

The kneading element used in the extruder pictured above. (Photo courtesy of Buss America)

clean and to maintain, and it can supply a constant flow of well developed dough over long periods of time. It can also be adapted to incorporate liquid flour preferments. Oxidation requirements for extruder-mixed doughs are similar to those of doughs mixed with a conventional horizontal mixer, and they are much lower than for doughs mixed with the old types of continuous mixers widely used during the 1960s.

Although the Amflow (AMF, Inc.) and the Do-Maker (J.C. Baker) continuous dough mixing systems are no longer available from their original manufacturers, they had a tremendous impact on dough-making technology during the early 1960s. Even though very few bakers still use this type of mixing equipment and continue to deposit the dough directly into baking pans, much of what is known today about dough conditioning and liquid flour preferments was learned in the early days of continuous mixing. Bakers have learned to overcome the problem of poor flavor development in continuously mixed bread by depositing the dough pieces, or a continuous ribbon of dough, onto a flour-dusted conveyor belt, thus producing a more "conventional" product with this equipment. The dough is then processed with conventional bread make-up equipment. These additional dough processing steps strengthen the gluten structure in the dough. The resulting baked loaves are in all aspects almost indistinguishable from bread prepared from doughs mixed in conventional batch mixers.

Vertical dough mixers are used for dough mixing only by small bake shops, such as retail and experimental bakeries. Except for the *dough hook* (mixing attachment), the retail baker uses the same mixer and mixing bowl for dough mixing and for mixing cake batters, icings, and fillings. The capacity of the mixing bowls ranges from 10 quarts (approximately 4 lb. or 2 kg dough) to 140 quarts (about 55

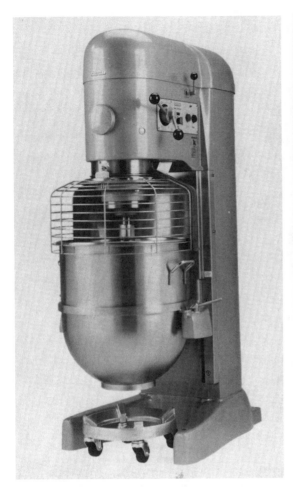
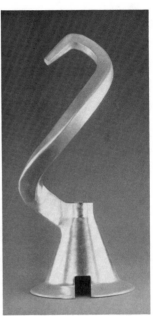

Left, a V-1401 vertical mixer. Above, an ED dough arm, or spiral dough hook, for a vertical mixer. (Photos courtesy of Hobart Corp.)

lb. or 24 kg dough). Each bowl size has its own size and type dough hook to develop the gluten in the dough. Except for the smaller bowls for each mixer size, the dough hooks are generally available in two different configurations. While only the straight "E" hooks are available for the smaller bowls, the larger bowls in each set can be fitted with either the straight "E" hook, or with the spiral "ED" mixing attachment. The spiral "ED" hook is generally preferred for mixing doughs, because doughs have a lesser tendency to "climb up" to the neck of spiral hooks than on straight hooks.

Right, a McDuffee bowl and pin mixer ready for use. Above, the McDuffee bowl and mixing attachment. (Photos above courtesy of National Manufacturing Co.

In an attempt to duplicate the efficient mixing action of horizontal mixers, a series of pin mixers was developed for use in baking laboratories. The McDuffee bowl has a flat bottom and a vertical pin at the center. The mixing attachment consists of two slightly curved prongs orbiting around the center pin with minimal clearance. Three-prong mixing attachments and water-jacketed mixing bowls for additional temperature control are also available. McDuffee bowls are available for Hobart 12 and 20 quart mixers from National Manufacturing (TMCO, Inc.) in Lincoln, Nebraska. The same company also manufactures small capacity pin mixers designed for flour evaluations.

Dividers

Mechanical dividers are used in bakeries to subdivide doughs into small pieces. Weight accuracy for the individual dough pieces is as important as not abusing the dough in the process.

Until the early 1980s, practically all dough dividers measured the dough by volume and were called *pocket dividers*. The number of pockets in such a divider ranged from one to eight. Reciprocating movements of the various parts in the divider limits the number of "cuts" per minute the divider can efficiently make. These dividers have one central adjustment for the "scaling weight" of all pockets. This requires the periodic calibration of every individual pocket to make sure that each deposits the same amount of dough. Because the dough in a batch continues to ferment between the start of the dividing process and its completion, it changes density, i.e., an equal volume of dough grows lighter as the yeast produces more and more leavening gas. This requires constant checking of the weight of individual dough pieces so that the necessary adjustments in the divider settings can be made. However, much of the problem of changing weights has been alleviated by cooler dough temperatures (73-75°F or 23-24°C) and with the introduction of a *degasser,* which is essentially a pump designed to expel accumulated fermentation gases from the dough immediately before it enters the divider hopper. The degasser keeps the dough density from changing significantly during the 20 to 30 minutes while the entire batch is processed by the divider.

In order to keep the labor cost for the production of bread as low as possible, productivity per man-hour is usually increased through higher production rates. Increased production rates often cause equipment problems. Reciprocating *pocket dividers* are not only built with more pock-

An AMF pocket divider, Baker Perkins (APV) rounder, and AMF intermediate (overhead) proofer.

ets, but they are often operated at a greater speed than recommended by the manufacturer of the equipment. This higher speed causes excessive wear in the equipment and larger deviations from the intended scaling weight. Equipment manufacturers responded to this problem by replacing the reciprocating pocket dividers, which were first introduced to the baking industry in 1901, with a new generation of dough dividers.

The *rotary divider* was developed in the early 1980s. This divider degasses the dough prior to extrusion through an orifice, where the pieces are cut off by two rotating plastic knives. By adjusting the speed of the dough pump and the revolutions per minute of the revolving cut-off knives, the operator is able to control the scaling weight of the dough

AMF Advanced Dough Divider.

An APV XD "J" Divider. (Photo courtesy of APV Baker, Inc.)

A Dutchess press divider/rounder.

in the range of 9-36 ounces (0.255 -1.020 kg) to a very high degree of accuracy.

Another relatively recent design, the *Series 'J' Divider*, utilizes two feeding rollers which degas the dough and feed it to a rotating measuring cylinder. This adjustable cylinder discharges the dough piece after approximately one half revolution onto a conveyor belt, which transports it to the dough rounder. The measuring cylinder on the opposite side of the piston is being refilled with fresh dough at the same time as the first dough piece is expelled by the piston.

The 'J' divider is designed to process a maximum of 19,800 lb. (9,000 kg) dough per hour for scaling weights ranging from 12-38 ounces (0.340-1.080 kg). This divider, too, is claimed to provide a very high degree of weight control. Since it operates under continuous positive pressure, it uses some divider oil only to lubricate the measuring cylinder, but not to seal the piston. This results in a significant reduction in the contamination of the dough with mineral oil.

Small retail shops and food service bakeries generally use *press dividers* which cut a scaled dough piece into a given number of smaller pieces of dough. Many of these semi-manual dividers can "round" the individual dough pieces so that these can be "panned" without further processing. Although most press dividers are configured for buns and rolls (36 dough pieces), some of the newer models can easily be converted to yield only six, nine, or 18 dough pieces. The six or nine unit dough presses are generally used for bread production.

Rounders

After dividing, dough pieces are usually "rounded." The rounding process smooths the dough surface and reduces the piece's surface area after dividing by shaping the dough piece into a tight round ball with a "dry" skin. In high-speed production, the rounding is done mechanically either with a conical dough rounder, or with a rounding bar (race) mounted above a moving conveyor belt. There are two types of conical rounders, the upright cone and the

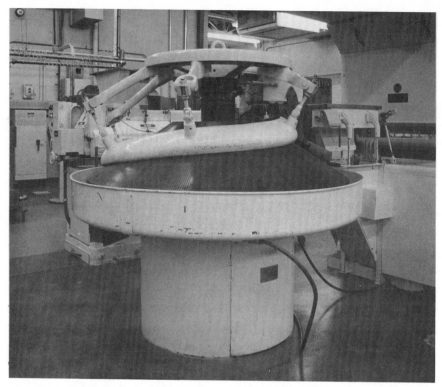

A Baker Perkins (APV) Rounder.

inverted cone. Both have grooved surfaces for improved traction for the dough pieces and a spiral rounding bar fitted to the cone. While the upright cone has the rounding mechanism on the outside, it is on the inside of the inverted cone. The freshly divided dough piece is picked up by the rounding bar at the bottom of the cone. It is then moved along by the rotating cone between its surface and the stationary rounding bar until it falls onto the transfer conveyor at the top, which transports it to the intermediate proofer.

The curvature and adjustment of the rounding bar and the scaling weight of the dough piece determine how well the dough piece is moulded into a round dough ball with a dry and smooth skin. When the rounding bar is too large for the dough piece or adjusted too loosely, the dough piece will not be properly "rounded." On the other hand, when the curvature of the rounding bar is too small for the dough piece, sticky dough may build up on the inside of the race, dough pieces may double up, and small dough shavings may be trimmed off some units and picked up by others, thus altering their weights.

There are no small-scale dough rounders available. Therefore, most retail bakers round their dough pieces by hand. However, some small bakers may use round bread moulders for rounding dough pieces. These moulders for shaping round breads consist of a conveyor with a straight rounding bar mounted diagonally over the moving belt. This equipment is excellent for moulding round bread after the rounded dough pieces have relaxed for a few minutes.

Intermediate Proofer

The purpose of intermediate proofers is to allow the rounded dough pieces to relax before they are degassed and moulded into loaves. Since this equipment is usually placed above some dough processing machinery, it is generally referred to as an *overhead proofer.*

Intermediate proofers consist of trays carrying the dough pieces through a cabinet, which protects the product from drying out. These cabinets are generally operated under ambient conditions, i.e. they are not heated and their humidity is controlled by the environment. The size of these intermediate proofers is usually large enough to allow the dough pieces a *rest time* of five to 15 minutes. This relaxation time is generally determined by the ambient conditions and the yeast level in the dough.

An APV intermediate proofer with two cross grain moulders. (Photo courtesy of APV Baker Inc.)

Bread Moulders

Bread moulders are used to shape the rested dough pieces into loaves. Although there are many different types of moulders available, the basic concept of mechanical moulding applies to all: the dough piece is first sheeted and degassed by a series of rollers. The flattened dough piece is then "curled" (rolled up) by passing under a flexible chain on a conveyor belt and moulded tightly between the moving conveyor belt and a stationary contoured "pressure board." The moulded dough piece is deposited into a baking pan, or onto proofing trays, either manually or automatically. The primary difference between the various types of moulders lies in how the dough piece is directed through the various moulding steps.

Straight Grain Moulder

A *straight grain moulder* passes the dough piece straight through the sheeting (head) rollers, the curling chain, and pressure board. The dough piece never changes direction. The pores in the crumb are elongated in the direction of the product flow, which is across the surface of the bread slice. This gives the bread the appearance of a more open grain structure. Also, since all the coalesced gas bubbles are concentrated on the trailing edge of the sheeted dough piece, the possibility of large holes near the crust or sidewalls of the slices is very likely. This type of bread moulder is ideal for stiff doughs and is used today mostly by bakeries producing heavy variety breads with low gas retention.

An Acme Rol-Sheeter-Moulder, Standard Model No. 88. (Photo courtesy of Acme, D.R. McCalin & Son)

Drum Moulder

The *drum moulder* operates like a straight grain moulder. However, this moulder is more compact and, for a long time, it was the preferred moulder in small bakeries. The main difference between the straight grain and the drum moulder is that in the drum moulder a rotating drum replaces the conveyor belt of the regular moulder. The pressure board is contoured around the outside of the drum. Because of the way this moulder is constructed, it is not suitable for automatic panning of dough pieces.

Cross Grain Moulder

The most commonly used moulder for white pan bread is the *cross grain moulder*. This moulder requires rather soft and extensible doughs. The descriptive name of this moulder comes from the fact that the direction of the moulding table (curling chain and pressure board) is perpendicular to the direction of the head rolls that degas and sheet the dough. As the flattened dough pieces move toward the moulding table with its conveyor belt moving at a right angle to the conveyor coming from the sheeting rollers, they are deflected onto the moulding conveyor for shaping into a loaf. The leading edge of the dough piece becomes one end of the loaf, and the trailing edge becomes the other end. Since the gas cells have been elongated from the leading to the trailing edge of the dough, i.e. from one end to the other end of the loaf, slicing the crumb will expose only the small cross section of the gas cells. This will give the impression of a tighter crumb grain, which the baker and the consumer tend to prefer.

Tendercurl Moulder

A variant of the cross grain moulder is the *tendercurl moulder*. This type of make-up requires a very relaxed and

A Peerless cross-grain moulder and panner. (Photo courtesy of Peerless Machinery Corp).

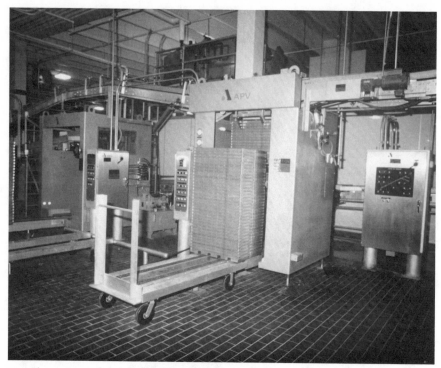

A pan stacker/unstacker. (Photo courtesy of APV Baker, Inc.)

extensible dough. This is generally achieved with a slightly higher dough water absorption and by properly conditioning the dough with mixing (full gluten development) and controlled fermentation.

The initial processing of the dough pieces is the same as with the cross grain moulder, except that the pieces are sheeted thinner and thus cover a larger surface area. After curling and moulding, this method produces a very long dough cylinder (about twice the length of a normal loaf) which then passes at an angle under a second curling chain on a moulding table placed perpendicular to the first moulding table which converts the long moulded dough piece into a shorter "twist" (much like a tight corkscrew) of the same length as the baking pan. Since the air cells in the crumb point in many directions, the grain of the crumb is

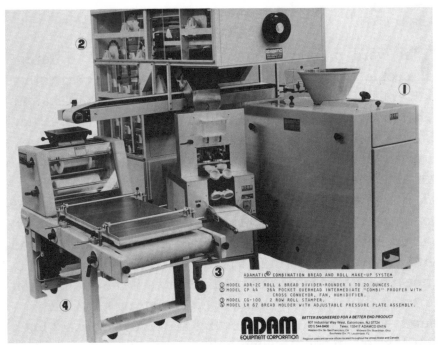

An Adamatic bread makeup system.(Photo courtesy of Adam Equipment Corp.)

slightly irregular and assumes the character of "old-fashioned" bread. The tendercurl make-up is a trademark for some "branded" bread.

Bread Panning

All moulders for large-scale bread production are equipped with automatic bread-panning devices. These attachments not only save labor cost, they also tend to "pan," or position, the loaves more uniformly in the bread pan. Moulders for small-scale production generally require that the dough pieces are panned manually. Many of the smaller moulders designed for retail or experimental bakeries are actually dough sheeters, which can be converted to moulders with attachments, e.g. a curling chain and an adjustable pressure board.

Proofers

The word *proofer* means different things to different people. Moreover, the spelling changes to *prover* in other parts of the English speaking world. Looking into Webster's Dictionary of the English Language does not help, either. Contrary to all definitions found in English dictionaries, *proofing* means to bakers in many other parts of the world "final fermentation," and the home baker calls it *"allowing the dough to rise."* Both terms are quite descriptive of the real process. The *proof time* is the period between moulding and panning of the dough piece and when it is placed into the oven for baking. It is, therefore, the last period of time when the yeast is allowed to ferment the dough (final fermentation) and to produce the leavening gas which expands the loaf volume (allowing the dough to rise) for a soft texture in the finished baked product.

Since enzymatic (yeast) reactions proceed at an accelerated rate at elevated temperatures, yeast-leavened products are generally allowed to "proof" to the desired size at a temperature higher than "normal" fermentation temperatures. The strength of the flour used for bread production and the strains of yeast used in this country make it possible to "proof" yeast-leavened products at temperatures between 104-115°F (40-46°C). However, European bakers prefer slightly lower temperatures for their products.

To better control the conditions for proofing the yeast leavened products prior to baking, the baker utilizes either a *proof box* or an *automated proofer.* Proof boxes are used primarily in conjunction with manually loaded ovens, while automated proofers also require automated loading and unloading facilities for ovens and bread coolers.

Whether the baker utilizes a proof box or an automated proofer, these facilities are used to control the environment

A proof box that will handle six racks.

for proofing yeast-leavened product. Depending on the product being processed, the temperature of proofing facilities is generally controlled within a range of 95-115°F (35-46°C). The relative humidity is adjusted to about 80-85% to prevent the formation of a dry crust on the dough pieces. This represents a temperature differential of 5-6°F between dry and wet bulb thermometers. Because of the cooling effect of evaporating moisture, the wet bulb thermometer, with its mercury reservoir covered with a wet cotton wick, normally indicates a lower temperature. The difference between dry and wet bulb temperatures diminishes as the surrounding air approaches moisture saturation, i.e., 100% relative humidity.

It is very important that the heat is properly distributed in the proofing facilities. This is more difficult in proof boxes than in automatic proofers. In the automated sys-

The photo above shows the proofer discharge of an automated Lanham System Continuous Proofer. Below is a Generation II Lanham Style Oven. (Photos courtesy APV Baker, Inc.)

tems, the product moves slowly on trays, racks, or conveyor through the proofer. A light air movement keeps the temperature relatively constant throughout the proofer, once the air-flow from the heat source has been properly adjusted. The enclosed system keeps the loss of heat to the outside environment at a minimum. This is in contrast to proof boxes. Here the product is placed on racks pushed gradually through the "box" from the entrance door to the exit door. Every few minutes, however, doors are opened to admit a new rack full of freshly panned product or to remove a rack to be transferred to the oven. Every time this happens, warm air and humidity is lost and replaced with cooler air, which accumulates at the bottom of the proof box. Therefore, the temperature in proof boxes (rack proofers) is seldom, if ever, uniform throughout. Product near the top of the rack may be overproofed, while the same product near the bottom of the rack may be underproofed. Much of this problem can, however, be alleviated with proper ductwork recirculating the air in the proofing chamber.

Proof boxes, however, give the baker flexibility. The baker is able to mingle products requiring different proof times and the baker is also better able to monitor the product while it is proofing. The sequence of racks to be loaded into the oven can also be rearranged, if this becomes necessary.

Small bakeries generally use *proof cabinets* or a small *rack proofer*, particularly when the baker also uses a rack oven for baking. The baker must only make sure that the rack for the oven also fits into his proof box. The proof cabinets, however, will usually only accept individual sheet pans or trays, which can serve as carriers for smaller pans.

To be functional, all proofers must be equipped with controls to regulate temperature and humidity. The humidity is usually produced with an electric heater in a water bath next to the heating element for the air, or it is introduced as atomized water spray or as low pressure steam together with the warm air used to keep the proofers at the desired temperature. The warm and humid air is evenly distributed throughout the proofing facility by ducts, which either recirculate the warm air from the top to the bottom, or feed new conditioned air continuously from the bottom and the cooler areas in the proofer.

Ovens

There is probably more variation in ovens than in any other equipment used by bakers. Although wood, peat, and coal are still used as oven fuel in other parts of the world, they are no longer of importance in the United States and Canada. The main oven fuel in North America is natural gas. Alternate sources for heat are electricity and regular heating oil. As a result of severe gas shortages in the mid-1970s, some bakeries have arrangements with their natural gas suppliers allowing them to shut off the gas after adequate warning has been given. Even though natural gas is no longer in short supply, many bakeries still keep a good supply of an alternate fuel like regular heating oil on hand for emergencies.

Gas Ovens

Most gas ovens are *direct fired ovens*. Combustion of the fuel takes place within the baking chamber. This, however, can only be the case when the combustion is "clean," i.e., the fuel leaves no significant amount of ash or odorous gases after combustion such as sulfur dioxide and similar impurities. Only highly refined gases and oils should be used for direct fired ovens. Therefore, oil-heated ovens are generally *indirectly fired ovens*, i.e., the combustion chamber is separate from the baking chamber. The heat from the combustion chamber is transferred to the baking chamber above it, either through the hearth separating the two chambers, or via a thermal oil, which picks up the heat at the point where it is generated and conveys it to the baking chamber at another location nearby. The first type of indirectly fired ovens evolved from the original dome-shaped brick ovens in about 1870 when the emerging larger commercial bakeries required continuously heated ovens. This was accomplished by the addition of a fire box for wood and coal burning below the baking hearth. However, this method still required skill for maintaining the proper heat in the baking chamber.

Direct-fired ovens returned to the baking industry when natural gas became the preferred fuel for generating oven heat. Clean natural gas consists primarily of methane, which turns into carbon dioxide and water upon combustion. It leaves no ashes or odors. With the electrification of this country during the first third of the 20th century, electricity became another source of clean energy, particularly in some of the remote agricultural areas. Today, primarily for economic reasons, natural gas is the number one choice of bakers, followed by electricity and other fuels. There are very few bakeries left in this country that still use wood or coal fired ovens. Today's issue for bakeries in the United States is primarily the fuel efficiency of ovens, as well as the control of pollution from oven exhaust.

There have been more changes in oven design during the past 100 years than during all previous history. The old domed brick ovens gave way to draw-plate and steel deck ovens. At the beginning of this century three major new designs appeared that are still in use today: the tunnel (traveling hearth) oven, the traveling tray (single lap and double lap) oven, and the reel oven which is very popu-

A reel oven.(Photo courtesy of Reed Oven Co.)

*A Winkler deck oven.
(Photo courtesy of Winkler
USA)*

lar in smaller shops. Single and multiple deck ovens are really only different versions of the original brick hearth ovens, since they are still loaded and unloaded with a peel (a flat wooden scoop).

Deck Ovens

The individual oven decks have their own temperature controls and can be heated either with electricity or with natural gas. Availablity of steam injection makes these ovens ideal for baking hearth breads such as French bread and Jewish rye bread.

Convection Ovens

During the 1960s and 1970s, convection ovens of all types and sizes appeared on the scene. They range from small

An electric rack oven.

An impingement oven. (Photo courtesy of Enersyst Development Center)

Ductwork for an impingement oven. (Photo courtesy of Enersyst Development Center)

cabinet ovens for food service operations to rotating rack ovens holding one double-rack full of bakery products. These ovens are named for the forced flow of heated air (convection) through the oven chamber. Since this airflow prevents the buildup of a layer of cooler air above the product, the heat reaches the bread, roll or cake more directly and efficiently. Convection ovens, therefore, tend to bake product faster and at a lower temperature (25-35°F or 14-19°C) than ovens depending on natural convection in the oven chamber.

Another type of small forced air oven, the impingement oven, utilizes an array of high-velocity hot air jets for increased heat penetration. These streams of hot air are aimed in a well defined pattern directly at the product being baked while it moves gradually through the oven.

Since forced air ovens bake at a lower temperature, they have the potential to be more energy efficient than other types of ovens, as long as they are well designed and insulated.

Oven Designs

Although all ovens utilize a variety of methods to transfer heat from its source (burner or electrical element) to the product being baked, most of these heat transfers are based either on contact with a hot surface (baking hearth), or on natural or induced convection of hot air (air blowers). Some heat is also radiated from the burners or from the walls of the baking chamber. Since radiation heat is absorbed proportionally to the area of the mass exposed to the radiation, very little infrared radiation heat is lost to the environment. New oven technologies utilize this property. Infrared gas burners, as well as electric infrared heating elements, are now available in ovens used by the fast-food restaurant trade.

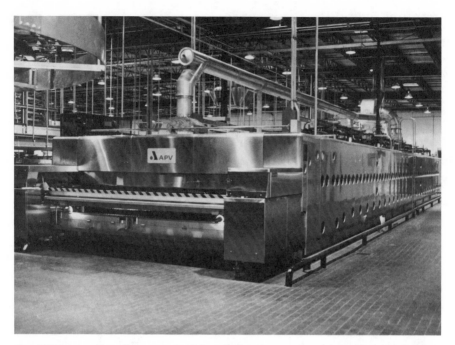

An APV traveling tray oven with pan loader and unloader. (Photo courtesy of APV Baker, Inc.)

Significant improvements were not only made in oven and burner design, but also in the oven controls. Any oven control is only as good as the location of the sensors in the oven and the adjustments that can be made by the oven operator. Ideally, the oven burners should only generate as much heat as the product absorbs during baking, plus the amount of energy lost to the pans and environment. If the burners provide much more heat than is consumed during the baking process, they tend to cycle between "on" and "off." The larger the difference between burner capacity and heat consumption, the more the temperature in the oven will fluctuate, or "override" the desired temperature, when the burners shut off during cycling. This fluctuation can lead to a very non-uniform bake, i.e., the crust color of product will constantly vary from light to dark.

Tunnel ovens and traveling tray ovens generally have

multiple heat zones, each regulated by individual controls. With these controls, the oven operator is not only able to adjust the temperature needed in every zone, but he can usually also control how much of the heat comes from above or below the baking hearth. When the control zones in directly fired gas ovens regulate more than one burner and these burners "cycle" too frequently, the baker may want to shut off one or more of the burners. Another option is to adjust the "modulation" of the burners, i.e., change the amount of gas flowing to the burners. This, however, should be done by a knowledgeable person who has a very good understanding of all the oven controls.

Another important adjustment is the one for lateral heat (heat distribution across the oven band or oven trays). If the heat is not uniform from one side of the oven to the other, then the product will not be baked the same on both sides of the oven, and thus will vary in crust color and moistness.

Steam in Ovens

Products baked without a pan and directly on the hearth of the oven need some steam. This steam should be available in relatively high volume, but of a low pressure (*wet steam*: 5 ± 2 lb. pressure per square inch). High pressure steam not only fails to give the expected effect, but it is also very dangerous to the oven operator. Moreover, when the steam pressure is greater than the gas line pressure, it will douse the fire by interfering with the gas flow in the burner. In addition, steam is very corrosive to the equipment and, consequently, steam ovens require much additional maintenance. Steam escaping from the oven carries with it other volatile components which tend to deposit as a smudgy brown film on all surfaces they come in contact with, thus creating a sanitation problem.

Auxiliary Equipment

As auxiliary equipment, some bakeries use waterjets to split the tops of proofed bread or rolls prior to baking. This equipment uses a thin stream of water under high pressure to cut the dough to the desired depth and without causing the partial collapse of proofed-up dough, as often experienced with dull knives or blades.

Tunnel and traveling tray ovens in automated bakeries are generally equipped with automatic pan or product loaders and unloaders.

Practically all depanners found in bakeries today use suction cups to lift the freshly baked loaves from their pans and to deposit them on a conveyor belt. The pan inverters, which dump the loaves onto a conveyor, are no longer in use. This type of equipment is not only slow and very noisy, but it also damages pans with prolonged use.

Bread Coolers

The purpose of bread coolers is to provide the necessary conditions for freshly baked product to cool to a temperature of 95°F (35°C) or less under sanitary conditions. The temperature of the "cooled" bakery product is actually of only secondary importance. Of greater importance is the fact that it takes time for the starch in the crumb to "set up" (stale) sufficiently to resist collapse during the slicing and packaging process. This staling process of the amylose fraction of the starch proceeds at a faster rate at lower temperatures. A "cooling time" of about 60 minutes under ambient conditions is generally adequate for pan breads, while 30 minutes suffices for buns and rolls, which are smaller and have a slightly lower moisture content.

Much of the energy absorbed by bakery foods during

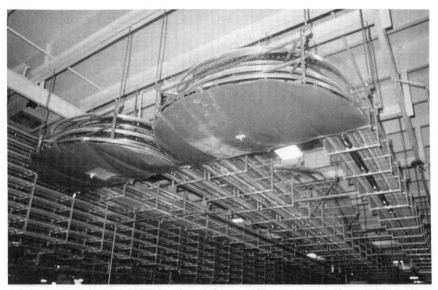

An overhead bread cooling conveyor. (Photo courtesy of APV Baker, Inc)

the baking process is released during cooling. While some of this energy is dissipated as heat by air movement, much of it is absorbed by the evaporating moisture escaping from the product. Since the ambient air has only a limited capacity to hold moisture, the rate of cooling for bakery foods depends not only on the ambient temperature, but also on the relative humidity in the room. During periods of low relative humidity or in dry climates, bread will cool more quickly than in a humid environment, even when the temperature is the same. If the product is cooled under dry conditions for longer than necessary to cool for packaging, it will dry out and thus lose some of its shelf-life. Therefore, in most areas of the United States and Canada, cooling time for bread products is much more critical in the winter than during humid summer days.

Proper cooling conditions are essential for the shelf-life of bakery foods. Baked products are nearly sterile when they are removed from the oven. All vegetative mold and all mold spores have been destroyed by the oven heat. Only few heat tolerant spores of some bacteria and wild yeast cells usually survive the baking process, and most of these are suppressed by inhibitors normally added to the dough by the baker. When bakers complain about a lack of shelf-life due to mold growth it is generally because of the exposure of their bakery food to a very large number of mold spores during the cooling stage. The source of this mold is either contaminated equipment or airborne particles.

Dirty cooling racks or conveyors can easily contaminate all bakery foods cooled on them with mold spores. If the cooler is in an enclosed room or adjacent to an uninsulated outside wall during the cold season the moisture in the warm air may condense on the cooler walls and will support mold growth.

Bakeries using unfiltered outside air to cool the bakery and the product, inadvertently "enrich" the environment with microbiological organisms, particularly on windy and humid days, or when dumpsters for waste materials are located near open windows and screened doors. No preservative prevents mold growth on bakery foods heavily contaminated with mold spores! Preservatives only "inhibit" mold growth slightly. Clean cooling facilities and filtered air in the cooling area can, however, prolong the mold-free life of bakery products much more effectively than any chemical preservative. While cooling racks must be washed periodically, cooling conveyors can and should be sanitized on a continuous basis. But the pads and gloves used by the bakery personnel, too, should not be forgotten. They are part of the total effort to keep the product free of mold.

Slicing and Packaging

There are three types of slicers used by the baking industry. Automated and larger bakeries generally use *band slicers.* Retail bakeries prefer to use the slower *reciprocating slicers* in their stores. *Rotary slicing machines*, the third type, are not very common in this country. They are used only to slice very dense bread such as Westphalian pumpernickel and loaves to be used for toasted or fried chips.

Band slicers have been developed for slicing very soft bread such as white pan bread. This equipment slices an entire loaf at one time. Band slicers employ a series of continuous blades with spacings between them controlled by a guide mechanism, which can be adjusted to give different slice thicknesses. The blades can be sharpened while in use. Dull blades tend to form "snow," an excessive amount of bread crumbs produced during slicing. Slicing crumbs are usually removed continuously by an air stream coming from an air compressor. This air, if not filtered, can be a source for severe mold contamination.

Reciprocating slicers are generally used by small bakeries for slicing individual loaves right in the store. Larger bakeries use these slicers for slicing raisin or other fruit breads, because the sugary fruit in these products tends to cause the build-up of a gummy residue on the blades. Reciprocating slicer blades are much easier to clean than the continuous slicing bands; but reciprocating slicers are much slower than band slicers and their mechanism makes them much noisier. In order to facilitate the slicing process, each reciprocating slicer has two sets of blades fixed in frames. While alternate blades move in one direction during the slicing process, the blades in between them move in the opposite direction. These movements are reversed during the following stroke. If the baker wants thicker or thinner slices, new sets of frames and guides for the knives must be installed. Most bakers do not sharpen dull knives for this type of slicer. They just replace them.

Whereas reciprocating slicers used to cause many accidents in the past, safety features on the newer models have significantly reduced the potential for such accidents. They are available as bench-top slicers for slicing individual loaves and as free standing units with a feeder which can hold a number of loaves at one time for semi-continuous slicing.

There are not many wrapping machines for bread left in use today. Most consumers appreciated the switch from wrapping paper to polyethylene or polypropylene bread bags, which help to protect the bread from drying out by being reclosable. The change to bread bags, however, forced bakeries to give up their quest for larger and larger bread loaves. While wrapping machines could adjust to varying loaf sizes, bread bags allow only minor variations in loaf volume. This makes it important for bakers using bread bags to produce the same size of bread consistently. Therefore, a good part of the responsibility for proper packaging

A reciprocating slicer.

An AMF bagger.

A Burford Tying machine in tandem with an AMF band slicer.. (Photo courtesy of the Burford Corp.)

is now shifted to the shoulders of production personnel, who control the size of the loaves. Bread bags also make it easier for the baker to comply with all the labeling regulations, since the respective display panels will always be in the same position.

The vast majority of automated bread bakeries use bagging machines operating on the same principle: they open the plastic bag automatically with a directed air stream and insert the sliced loaf into the bag by either pulling the opened bag over it, or by pushing the loaf into the opened bag.

Small bakeries unable to afford an automatic bagging machine prefer to use a bagging device which opens the polyethylene bag with an air stream, but which requires the operator to push the bread loaves through spring-loaded gates of a chute into the bag. This device is quite efficient in its operation and a skilled operator is able to attain very high production rates.

Although some retail bakeries still use hand-twisted wire ties, most bakeries now use tyers or a machine to close the bags with plastic clips. The twist ties are available in seven colors to denote every day of the week. Many bakers also use the principle of color coding with their plastic clips. These color codes do not indicate the day of manufacture, but they let the salesman know, on which day of the week the product must be removed from the shelves in the store for quick sale in the bakery's thriftstore. Other bakeries print dates on the clips, particularly in states requiring food manufacturers to indicate when their product can no longer be considered "fresh."

Summary

This brief review of equipment used by bakeries for the manufacture of bread products is not intended to be "complete." It is only meant to be an overview for those readers who like to know why bakeries in this country prefer one type of equipment over another. Even though it is not always apparent, there have been significant changes in bread-making equipment and technology since World War II and more progress is expected during the next decades. Many bakers used to start their career simply by asking for a menial job. The baker in the next century will be expected to know basic food chemistry and baking science, computer programming, and government regulations. Rather than being one of many poorly rewarded bakery workers, the baker of the future will be one of few well trained and remunerated specialists. Computer hookups may even enable him to control the production of many bakery foods from his home, while a minimum number of engineers and specialists will keep the plant serviced.

CHAPTER FOUR

Primary Ingredients for Bread

There are three major guidelines for the selection of any ingredient, such as flour or shortening: the ingredient must be functional, economical to use, and the supplier must back the quality of the ingredient with good service.

All three conditions are equally important and must be met satisfactorily. If the ingredient is a compound (two or more components) and an alternative to a presently used item, it must be very similar in composition or it will require changes in ingredient and nutrition labeling whenever the new ingredient is used interchangeably with the original item.

Flour

Flour is the most basic ingredient in all bread-like products. The type of flour used by the baker can vary not only according to its source: wheat, rye, barley, corn (maize), oats, amaranth, millet, etc., but also with respect to its grind or physical shape: fine or medium grind flour, cracked or flaked grains, and in the way it is refined or separated from unwanted components of the grain: patent flour, straight grade flour, whole meal. The type of grain product used in the manufacture of bread will not only affect the taste and texture of the baked product, but also the technology used and the final shape and size of the food. The reason why corn masa is baked in the shape of a tortilla, rather than in a loaf, is the total absence of a structure forming protein in corn. This structure forming protein found only in wheat is called *wheat gluten*. Proteins present in other grains are often called *gluten*, too, but these proteins do not form a three-dimensional cell structure, like wheat gluten does. Corn gluten, a by-product in the manufacture of corn starch and corn syrup, is not suitable for bread dough formation and is generally used as an animal feed.

Flour Quality

In the United States and Canada, the most suitable and commonly used flour for the manufacture of bread or bread-like bakery foods is milled from hard wheat grown in the region located between the Missouri River in the east, the Rocky Mountains in the west, and in the Canadian provinces north of this area. The dry climate in this region is ideal for the formation of the two wheat flour protein components which make up gluten when the flour milled from this wheat is blended with water and subjected to mechanical energy (mixing). Generally, the wheat grown in the southern states of this hard wheat region has a lower protein content than the wheat cultivated in the northern states. Winter wheat grown in northwest Texas, Oklahoma, Kansas, eastern Colorado, southern Nebraska and eastern South Dakota is planted in the fall and harvested in late spring or early summer. Spring wheat, grown in eastern Montana, North Dakota, and western Minnesota is sown in the spring and harvested in late summer or early fall. While some of the white wheat grown in Washington, Oregon, and Idaho is milled for local consumption, much of it is exported.

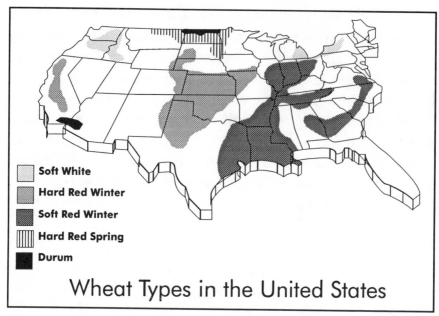

Soft White

Hard Red Winter

Soft Red Winter

Hard Red Spring

Durum

Wheat Types in the United States

This map shows the distribution of wheat growing areas by the types of wheat grown.

Until the advent of continuous bread dough mixing, flour milled from spring wheat, which is also known as "northwest wheat flour" with a protein content of normally 12% or more, was clearly preferred over the "southwestern wheat flour" milled from winter wheat with a protein content of usually less than 12%. Over the years, the protein content of a typical bread flour used by the wholesale baking industry dropped from 12.5-12.75% in the 1950s, to 11.75-12.25% twenty years later, and to the even lower level of 10.8-11.5% frequently found in bread flours today. Flours with a higher protein level are still used today, but only by small retail bakers or for the production of specialty bread products.

As the protein level of bread flour decreased over time, the amount of ash in the flour increased dramatically from about 0.42-0.44% in the 1970s to 0.48-0.51% twenty years later. Even though every miller will tell bakers that the ash content in the flour has no detrimental effect on the bread quality, the ash content does reflect the increased amount of flour the miller "extracts" from 100 pounds (lbs.) of wheat. In normal growing years, a miller is now able to get a yield of about 74 lbs. of flour from every 100 lbs. of wheat grist (grain mix prepared for grinding or milling), instead of the 72 to 73 lbs. of flour the miller extracted from the same amount of wheat 20 years ago. With new milling techniques, the miller is now able to separate the wheat germ and the bran from the wheat kernel with less loss of the adjacent endosperm, or starchy interior of the wheat kernel. Since the ash and protein contents of the endosperm increase from the center of the kernel to the outside, and the gluten quality of the protein tends to decrease in the same direction, a flour with the same protein content, but a higher ash content, may not be of as good a baking quality as a similar flour with a lower ash content.

But there were also other changes occurring at the same time. Forty years ago farmers were primarily interested in wheat varieties with a relatively high yield per acre under all types of growing conditions and with a good resistance to disease. Due to the effort of the Wheat Quality Council, a major effort is now being directed to breeding wheat cultivars (varieties) with a higher protein content and with a better bread making quality. This has paid off to such an extent that many major bread bakers today use flour milled from predominately hard red winter wheat.

The baking industry still maintains, and rightfully so, that the quality of bread flour today is not quite as good as it was before the 1980s. The real reason for this phenomenon seems, however, to be economics and not inability of the milling industry to provide bakeries with high quality flour. Mills feel compelled to respond to the wishes of purchasing agents in bakeries and supply them with lowest cost flour that meets minimum specifications. These specifications are changing almost every year with variations in the quality of the wheat crop. Unfortunately, the attempt to keep flour prices as low as possible has, over time, led to an erosion of flour quality.

How has the baker in the production department coped with changing flour quality all these years? New developments in bread ingredient technology provide bakers with dough strengtheners and dough oxidants which make the flour perform better and as if it has a higher protein content. Improvements in dough processing and in pan construction also help weaker doughs overcome the physical abuse experienced by fully proofed loaves prior to baking. However, the nice and "silky" texture of bread sold 30 and 40 years ago can rarely be found in today's product. Although most bread on the market now has been formulated with much consideration given to the health of the consumer by using ingredients such as polyunsaturated vegetable oil, no cholesterol, increased nutritional fiber content, "natural," "no preservatives," etc., the prime concern of the baker still seems to be the eye appeal of the bread and what can be claimed on the package, and not how the palate of the consumer is pleased.

The very long shelf-life built into commercial bread today has done very little or nothing to increase bread consumption. While freshly baked bread and products with a relatively short shelf-life, such as French bread, have gained much new interest in the consumer market, standard white pan bread is often considered only as a "platform" for other and more tasty food components. A bakery considering the taste of bread as important as its appearance will have a better chance for increased sales than a bakery concentrating solely on making the cheapest bread possible. The success of in-store bakeries in supermarkets is based on the sale of fresh bakery foods, rather than on keeping their bread products "edible" (i.e., soft and mold-free) for as long as possible.

Selection of Flour

The functionality of wheat flour in the formulation is of utmost importance. The quality of the finished product depends on how the wheat protein is developed into a three-dimensional gluten matrix which entraps carbon dioxide during fermentation and forms the cell structure supporting the product. This cell structure affects bread volume, texture and shelf-life.

In general, the miller and flour broker can best recommend which type and brand of flour is most suitable for a given application. The availability of a wide range of wheat flour in this country and the competition between mills favor the baking industry. Any bakery buying in truckload quantitites in bags or in bulk can choose the flour it deems best for its products. The only limiting factor will be cost, including the cost of transportation. However, the baker must always keep in mind that the "cheapest" ingredient is seldom the most economical ingredient! Losses incurred through the production of inferior or unsatisfactory bakery foods, or the use of expensive additives to correct deficiencies of "cheap" ingredients, can easily outweigh the gains obtained by buying a low-cost, but inferior flour.

Specifications for Bread Flour

Most ingredient specifications used by bakeries are written by the ingredient suppliers and not by the baker. For this reason, ingredient specifications are merely a description of what the vendor is able to supply to meet the baker's needs. Generally, samples fitting the description in the specification had previously been test-baked under normal manufacturing conditions and were found to function as desired by the baker. The physical and compositional description of the test-sample became then, almost automatically, its "specification" by simply replacing single numbers with ranges or with limiting values. In most cases, this method is adequate. Other competing suppliers frequently will provide similar, but still different, sets of specifications for ingredients to be used interchangeably with the first product. Because mills often buy the wheat they mill in different growing areas, it is not always easy for them to match flour functionality exactly with all the specification values of another mill, unless the baker is willing to pay a premium price. Therefore, specifications for ingredients may vary slightly from supplier to supplier and, sometimes, also from crop year to crop year.

Each ingredient specification consists of two major sections:

    a. Section written by the vendor (manufacturer or broker), and
    b. Section written by the user (bakery).

In the case of flour, the vendor will usually supply the information in the following areas:

    1. Analytical:
        Moisture content range or maximum value
        Protein content range
        Ash content range
        Alpha-amylase activity range
        Starch damage (if requested)
        Particle size (if requested)
    2. Rheological:
        Absorption (% of water absorbed by flour)

Mixing requirement
Tolerance of flour to mixing
3. Microbiological:
Total count of microbes per gram of flour
Count of mold spores
Count of wild yeast cells

The bakery generally will, or should, specify the following conditions:

1. **Flour must produce consistent results from shipment to shipment and must perform like approved initial production sample!**
2. Flour must/must not be enriched with vitamins and minerals to specified standard levels.
3. Flour must be milled, stored, and delivered to the bakery under sanitary conditions.
4. No extraneous matter in the flour beyond limits set by government regulations.
5. Flour must be delivered to the bakery as scheduled and specified (in bulk or bags).

There may be additional instructions in the specifications, such as flour treatment, the type of wheat used for the flour, and specific performance test requirements. When the bakery takes delivery of an entire truckload at a time, the bakery may request copies of analytical and test data for that particular flour shipment. Also, every specification value should be given with the respective testing method with which these results are obtained. A sample of a typical specification sheet for regular bread flour is given in Table I.

The average baker should really not be concerned with the numbers or values stated in the specification; nor should

Table I
Ingredient Specification

Premium Bread Company, Inc. Preparer: Jane B. Baker
Ingredient: Pan Bread Flour Ingredient Code: 101120
Date Issued: August 27, 1993
Date Approved: September 8, 1993 By: Joe M. Overhead
Last Revision:

Ingredient Description: Bakery flour milled from sound hard red winter wheat or from a blend of such wheat and hard red spring wheat.
Appearance: Flour must have a clean and white appearance.
Odor and Taste: No unusual off-odor or off-taste.
Packaging: Bulk shipment in tanker truck or railcar.

Analytical Values:	Standard	Test Method
Moisture %	13.5 ± 0.5	AACC 44-15A
Protein (14% M.B.*) %	11.5 ± 0.5	AACC 46-12
Ash (14% M.B.) %	0.49 ± 0.02	AACC 08-01
Starch Damage %	7.0 ± 2.0	AACC 76-30A

* 14% Moisture Basis (calculated for a 14% moisture content)

Rheological Performance:		Test Method
Dough Water Absorption %	59.5 ± 2.0	AACC 54-21
Arrival Time, minutes	2.0 ± 0.5	AACC 54-21
Peak Time, minutes	7.5 ± 1.5	AACC 54-21
Departure Time, minutes	15.0 ± 2.0	AACC 54-21
Stability Time, minutes	13.0 ± 2.5	AACC 54-21
Mixing Tolerance Index, BU	30.0 ±10.0	AACC 54-21

Alpha Amylase Activity:		
Amylograph Viscosity, BU	500.0 ±50.0	AACC 22-10
or Falling Number, seconds	220.0 ±20.0	AACC 56-81B

Flour Treatment:
All flour is to be bleached with benzoyl peroxide and treated with 10 parts per million azodicarbonamide to enhance its performance.

Extraneous Matter:	None	AACC

Microbial Contamination:		
Total Count	< 50,000/gram	BAM
Salmonella	Negative	BAM
E. Coli	< 10/gram	BAM
Yeast	<250/gram	BAM
Mold	<1000/gram	BAM

Enrichment:	Nutrient:	mg/100g Flour
	Thiamin (Vitamin B1)	0.64
	Riboflavin (Vitamin B2)	0.40
	Niacin (Vitamin B3)	5.30
	Iron, Reduced	4.40
	Calcium	212

these values be used as a legal basis for confrontations with the supplier. The only interest the baker should have is that the flour, or any other ingredient, conforms with government regulations for potential adulteration and that it functions properly in formulations and without drastic changes in the technology used in the plant. Also, the flour or ingredient must not in any way present a health hazard to employees or customers. An ingredient specification should also not give the supplier a license to ship to the baker an inferior product which still meets most or all specifications. A typical example for such a product would be a flour contaminated with heat-stable microorganisms which produce an off-color and/or a foreign aroma in the bread crumb. The federal government has established guidelines for maximum allowable levels of toxins in flour from pesticides and mold (aflatoxin and vomitoxin: 1 ppm). These guidelines are generally more of a concern to the miller than to the baker.

When flour is shipped in bags, the baker should specify the net weight in the bags and the number of bags stacked on a pallet. More and more bakers prefer to restack shipments of bagged product onto their own sanitized pallets in order to avoid the importation of insects and rodents into their premises. The baker may also request submission under separate cover of lot numbers and other manufacturing information for the flour received.

Performance Testing of Flour

There are two philosophies regarding testing of flour for performance. Users of large quantities of flour generally insist on testing a sample from every shipment of flour for its performance in white pan bread. A technician usually evaluates the dough rheology of the flour with one of the following instruments:

- Farinograph (Brabender)
- Alveograph (Chopin)
- Mixograph (TMCO National Mfg. Co.)
- Rheograph (Interstate Brands Corp.)

Standardized flour testing procedures have been developed for all instruments except the Rheograph. All instruments give reproducible results, which are generally recorded continuously as graphs. While the Alveograph measures the ability of a dough piece to stretch into a bubble under controlled conditions, the graphs produced by the other three instruments reflect changes in the torque exerted by the dough's viscosity on the shaft of the mixing attachment.

Since the configuration of the mixing bowl and the mixing attachment is different in each instrument, the graphs produced by them differ significantly. Farinograms and alveograms are relatively easy to interpret, but it takes some experience to properly evaluate the rheograms and mixograms. Each of these four instruments has advocates and critics and they will all indicate any significant changes in the flour quality and in the amount of water needed to form an extensible dough.

Farinograph

The Brabender Farinograph is the most popular dough rheology instrument used for measuring dough-making properties of flour, because the farinograms are relatively easy to interpret. Newer models of this instrument can also be interfaced with computers. Although none of the data can be applied directly to the manufacture of bread, they do provide valuable guidelines for formulating and mixing doughs. The dough water *absorption* indicates how much water must be added to the flour in order to obtain a dough of a desirable viscosity. For bread flour, the viscosity curve

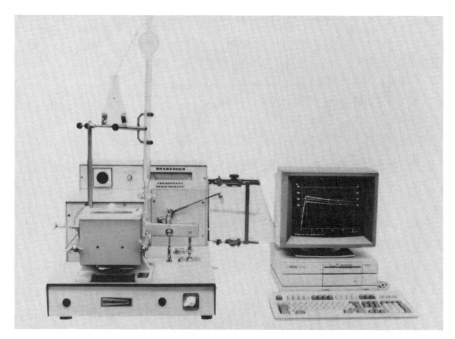

A Farinograph. (Photo courtesy of C.W. Brabender Instruments, Inc.)

is usually centered on the 500 BU line at its peak. The *arrival time* indicates how quickly the flour hydrates (pick-up time) and the *peak time* tells us how fast the dough "develops," i.e., the gluten forms. The *dough stability* time indicates the tolerance of the dough to mixing, while the Mixing Tolerance Index (MTI) indicates how fast the dough breaks down when it is overmixed.

Mixograph

The Mixograph is a small pin mixer for doughs with a recording device or a computer attached to it. It requires more experience for the proper interpretation of the parameters. The proper absorption (dough viscosity) is interpreted from the width and regularity of the recorded graph. The *peak time* is related to the time needed to develop the gluten structure in the dough, and the height of the peak is one of the indicators for the bread-making quality of the

The Farinogram provides valuable guidelines for formulating doughs, including water absorption, arrival time, and peak time.

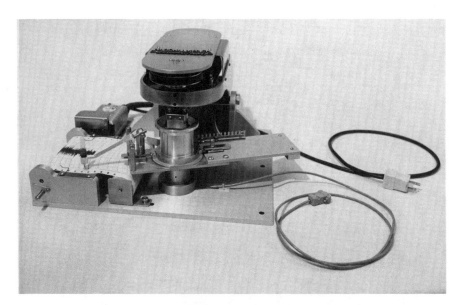

A Mixograph. (Photo courtesy of National Manufacturing, TMCO)

wheat protein in the flour sample. Lines drawn through the middle of the curves before and after the peak and intersecting at the peak, form the *dough strengthening angle*, which gives an indication of flour strength. The angle between the line drawn through the intersect and parallel to the baseline and the line drawn through the middle of the curve after the peak is called the *dough weakening angle*. A relatively large dough weakening angle (i.e., a steep descent of the curve after the peak) implies that the dough lacks tolerance to overmixing. Therefore, a good strong bread flour has relatively wide bands in the mixogram and the curve shows only a mild downward slope after it has reached its peak.

Alveograph

The Alveograph is widely used in Europe and is based on a different principle. Where the Farinograph and Mixograph measure changes in dough viscosity during extended mixing, the Alveograph mixes the dough with a

An indication of flour strength is provided by the dough strengthening angle and dough weakening angle on the Mixogram.

constant absorption (76% of total flour solids with flour moisture as part of the standard 76% absorption) and for a standard time. The developed dough is then extruded, sheeted and cut into patties which, after a predetermined amount of rest time, are subjected to air pressure which blows the dough patty into a bubble until it bursts. The instrument records the initial resistance of the dough to expansion (P), the extensibility of the dough (L), and the total amount of energy (W) absorbed by the dough during the bubble formation. It is claimed that these three indicators and the ratio P/L predict the ability of an actual bread dough made from this flour to form a grain (cell) structure with thin cell walls and a large volume.

Rheograph

The Rheograph is actually a Hobart A-200 mixer with a McDuffee bowl (a mixing bowl with a flat bottom and a fixed pin in the center and a two-prong dough developer orbiting around the center pin in the bowl). The mixer is

An Alveograph.

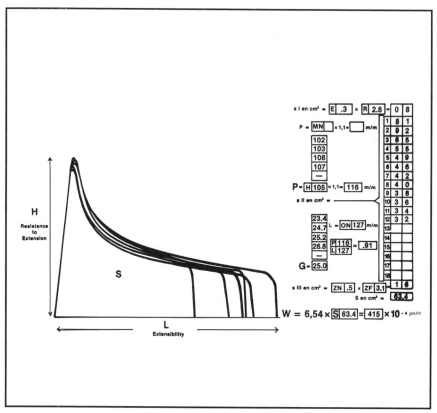

An Alveogram.

situated in an air conditioned cabinet and the torque on the mixing shaft is recorded as a vertical straight curve which gradually becomes narrower. The end point of this test is the total breakdown of the dough structure, or the *fatigue time*, measured in minutes.

Flour Testing at a Bakery

Some bakery laboratories also test-bake some or all of the flour samples submitted by the mills prior to shipping the load. But it is a rare case when the bakery's laboratory consistently approves the pre-shipment flour sample before the flour is unloaded at the bakery.

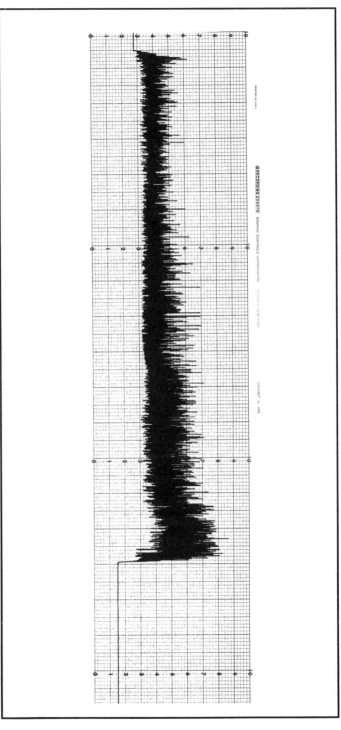

The Rheogram demonstrates the fatigue time of a dough.

The inability of a bakery laboratory to evaluate all submitted flour samples in time gives rise to much criticism from bakery production management. Usually, as time goes on, more and more flour shipments will be used in production before their representative samples are fully evaluated. Flour quality problems generally surface more frequently when millers start using wheat from a new crop year. Then top priority is again given to flour testing until everything has stabilized and the flour testing technician needs some time to catch up with other chores.

Because of the "after the fact" availability of flour testing data and the high cost of staffing and maintaining a good flour testing laboratory, many bakery managers consider an in-house flour testing program an unnecessary expense.

It is very useful to have a baking laboratory available for checking potential problems with ingredients or to identify the source of a production problem. Most bakeries cannot afford to duplicate the testing already done on a continuous basis by their flour supplier. All mills are anxious to provide bakers with the best flour the baker is willing to pay for and all mills have good quality assurance programs which require periodic testing of the flour being shipped to their customers. They will, therefore, be more than happy to provide any customer buying a truckload or more of their flour with copies of testing data for that specific lot of flour. If a baker does not trust the miller, the baker should search for one who instills confidence and who can supply a good performing flour on a continuous basis. Nobody will do well in business when the supplier of the main ingredient cannot be trusted. As the baker's product quality depends on the quality of ingredients purchased, the cooperative relationship with the flour supplier and miller is often the basis for the bakery's success or failure. Any good business relationship rests on the premise that every contract must be beneficial to both parties!

Flour Additives

Additives are added to flour for three different reasons: vitamin and mineral enrichment; improvement of flour performance; and improvement of flour appearance.

While the first two types of additives can also be added directly to doughs at the bakery, the bleaching process for the flour takes time and must be accomplished before the flour is used as an ingredient.

Flour Enrichment

The need to enrich bakery products with vitamins (thiamin, niacin, and riboflavin) is no longer as important as it was when the enrichment program was initiated to eliminate the deficiency of these three vitamins in the American diet before and during World War II. Many nutritional experts agree today that enriching flour and bread with these B-vitamins is no longer necessary. Others advocate the inclusion of folic acid into this program. Listing thiamin, niacin, and riboflavin is no longer required by the Food and Drug Administration in the new Nutrition Labeling and Education Act of 1990 (NLEA), unless enrichment with vitamins is part of a nutritional claim.

The Code of Federal Regulations for *enriched bread and rolls* (21 CFR Ch. I Part 136.115) requires that "..each such food contains in each pound 1.8 milligrams of thiamin, 1.1 milligrams of riboflavin, 15 milligrams of niacin, and 12.5 milligrams of iron." The requirements for *enriched flour* are that "...it contains in each pound 2.9 milligrams of thiamin, 1.8 milligrams of riboflavin, 24 milligrams of niacin, and 20 milligrams of iron."

While calcium is an optional enrichment ingredient, the

NLEA requires that the amount of calcium in a serving of food be declared as *% Daily Reference Value* (DRV). The DRV is based on the recommended daily intake of the nutrient component for an adult, which is one gram or 1000 milligrams (mg) calcium per adult.

The quantity of iron added to wheat flour as enrichment is based on the amount of this element lost when wheat is milled into white flour. Iron may be added either as *reduced iron* (electrolytic iron or iron reduced with hydrogen), or as a salt of inorganic or organic acids, such as ferrous sulfate, ferric orthophosphate, and ferrous fumarate. Iron, too, must be listed on the required label as % DRV, which has been established as 18 milligrams (mg) per adult.

Flour Improvers

Since much of the flour used by bread bakers is now shipped in bulk and used within a few days after milling, the flour no longer has the time to "age" at the mill or in the bakery. The aging of flour was once considered essential for its proper performance. During aging, flour absorbed oxygen from the air which resulted in a beneficial modification of the protein in the flour. Old time bakers took advantage of this phenomenon and stored their flour in woven cotton bags for three to four weeks in a room with good air circulation. Some of them even restacked the flour bags periodically, so that the bags came into contact with fresh air. The bakers also noted that three or four days after the flour was milled, there was a period of five to seven days when the flour produced sticky doughs and small loaves. They referred to this period as the *sweating period* and the unaged flour was called "green flour."

Maturing Agents

As bakeries grew larger and their daily usage of very large quantities of flour made the storage and handling of flour in bags impractical, millers started to add chemical oxidizing agents to the flour to eliminate the long storage time during which the flour was allowed to *age* naturally. Although chlorine dioxide and nitrogen trichloride were widely used to age flour during the early years of flour treatment, these chemicals are no longer used in the United States and they have been replaced primarily with 5-10ppm azodicarbonamide (ADA) added to white flour milled from hard red winter wheat, or with 10-20 ppm potassium bromate in white flour milled from hard red spring wheat. Bakers and millers are now encouraged by the Food and Drug Administration to discontinue the use of potassium bromate for the manufacture of bakery foods, and some millers have started to substitute 20-40 ppm ascorbic acid (AA) or blends of ascorbic acid and ADA for potassium bromate. Iodates and other potential flour oxidants, too, have been investigated for this purpose.

While the addition of potassium bromate to flour must be declared as such in the ingredient statement, azodicarbonamide is legally declared as a *bleaching agent*, even though it has no whitening effect on flour.

While Canada limits the amount of ascorbic acid in flour to 200 ppm, there is currently no restriction on its addition to flours milled in the United States. Even though ascorbic acid is also known as Vitamin C, the baker cannot claim the addition of this vitamin since Vitamin C loses its vitamin function during dough processing and baking. In fact, the baker does not need to declare any addition of this dough improver since it is considered to be merely a processing aid and not a component of the finished product.

Enzymes in Flour

Millers are generally requested to standardize the alpha-amylase activity in flours used for the production of yeast-raised (yeast-leavened) bakery foods. The natural alpha-amylase activity in wheat flour varies with the climatic conditions which existed when the wheat was harvested. When the weather is very warm and dry at harvest time, the wheat and the flour milled from it will have a very low alpha-amylase activity. Conversely, when wet weather delays the harvest of mature wheat, the sprouting process begins in some of the kernels, especially in those which have absorbed much moisture and are prevented from drying out rapidly after the rain has stopped.

Sprouting, or germination, depends on the formation and activation of many enzymes in the seed. Alpha amylase is one of these enzymes which help convert the starch in the wheat kernel to sugar and energy needed for the germ to grow into a plant. Even though sprouting is a desirable trait in a seed, the presence of an excessive amount of enzymes formed during this process detracts from the baking quality of the flour milled from *sprout damaged* wheat. However, some alpha-amylase activity in the flour is desirable, since it provides fermentable sugars for the yeast, particularly in flour preferments like liquid or plastic sponges.

Unless the baker prefers an untreated flour, millers generally standardize the flour with diastatic (containing amylase enzymes) barley malt to an alpha-amylase activity of 450 to 550 Brabender Units (BU), when measured with a Brabender Viscograph (Amylograph), or to a range of 225 to 275 seconds with the Falling Number instrument.

Both instruments measure the viscosity of a standard starch or flour paste heated at a controlled rate. The Falling Number instrument does this much more quickly than

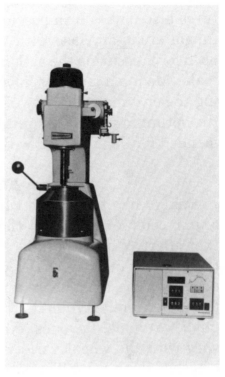

Above, a falling number apparatus. Right a Visco/Amylo/Graph PT 100. (Photo at right courtesy of C.W. Brabender Instruments, Inc.)

the older Amylograph. The values obtained with either instrument vary inversely with the alpha-amylase activity, i.e. a higher value in BU (Brabender Units on Amylogram) or in seconds (Falling Number) will indicate a lower amylolytic activity. This is because the value produced by either instrument reflects the viscosity of the flour-water paste, which decreases as the alpha amylase breaks down the starch paste.

Although the American milling and baking industries still prefer to use barley malt for standardizing the alpha-amylase activity in bread flours, millers in most other countries prefer the use of similar enzymes from a fungal source. The thermal death point (temperature, at which the enzymes are inactivated) of fungal amylase is about 10-15°F (5-8°C) lower than for cereal (malt) amylase. This difference in the sensitivity of the enzymes to elevated temperatures also makes it impossible to measure the activity of fungal alpha-amylase with the standard methods developed for measuring the activity of enzymes found in barley malt. Modified methods have been developed for measuring the enzymatic activity of fungal enzymes in flour, but the optimum values are quite different from those recommended for flour treated with cereal amylase.

Flour Bleaching

Bakers like to produce white breads with a very light crumb color, even though they no longer make claims to that effect. Wheat contains naturally yellow pigments in the starchy interior of the wheat kernel, called the endosperm. These pigments tend to impart a yellowish tint to the flour milled from it. The types of pigments (xanthophyll, carotene, flavones, etc.) and the amounts present vary with the wheat variety. When the baker specifies a bleached flour, the miller will treat the flour with a *bleaching agent* to destroy the pigments. The bleaching process takes place by oxidation of "unsaturated carbon chains" (containing a double bond between two adjacent carbon atoms) in the coloring bodies.

The most effective and widely used bleaching agent for bread flours is *benzoyl peroxide*. Its action is not instantaneous and it requires several days before the bleaching action is complete. The "normal" application rate for this treatment agent, a solid, is about 50 ppm; but it may vary from 30 to 100 ppm, depending on the wheat variety. Benzoyl peroxide has no maturing effect on the flour and it is, therefore, often used in combination with ADA, which has no bleaching effect. Whether the flour is treated with one or with both of these oxidizing agents, it must be labeled as "bleached."

Another bleaching agent is *chlorine dioxide*. This flour treatment agent is really a better maturing agent than a bleaching compound for flour pigments. Chlorine dioxide has been used since 1948, primarily for all-purpose flours. It is added to the flour at a rate of about 15 ppm.

Wheat Flour Types

Besides the regular bread flour described previously in this chapter, there are other wheat flour types available to the baker. With the advent of roller mills, the miller is able to separate the products of different milling steps into separate *streams* which he can recombine to flours of different baking qualities.

Milling of Flour

The overall flour quality is determined by two major phases of milling:

1. Extraction of flour from the wheat.
2. Separation and recombination of flour streams.

Flour Extraction

White flour is produced by *extracting* as much of the starchy part of the grain kernel as possible by removing the bran coat and the germ from the *stock* (broken up grain). The *extraction rate* of flour (pounds of flour recovered from 100 lb. wheat) depends on several factors:

1. Milling quality of the wheat.
2. Milling technology used.
3. Relative cost of flour and mill feed.
4. Moisture content of wheat.

For many years, the extraction rate for wheat averaged about 72%. However, since the late 1970s, millers started to gradually increase this rate until they now recover up to 76 lbs. of flour from 100 lbs. of wheat. The remainder consists of bran, wheat germ, and *shorts* (a mixture of bran, germ, and flour). Although some of the bran and wheat germ is recovered for human consumption, most of it is sold with the shorts as animal feed.

The price for mill feed has a significant effect on the cost of flour and, to a lesser extent, also on the flour quality. If the price for mill feed is relatively high, then the miller can sell the flour at a slightly lower price. Conversely, when the miller receives very little for the mill feed fractions, then flour prices rise to offset the milling cost. This market condition will also induce the miller to extract more flour from the grist and to produce less mill feed.

Flour Separation

With the advent of roller mills, the miller is able to separate the extracted flour into different *streams,* or fractions of flour produced by the various milling steps, which the miller selectively recombines to obtain flour of a specified quality.

Millers can *separate* their flours into two groups: *patent flour* and *clear flour*. While the patent flour comes from the innermost parts of the endosperm in the wheat kernel, the clear flour comes from the outer portion of the endosperm. Depending on how much clear flour the miller withholds from the patent flour, the miller can produce a variety of patent and clear flours. By combining all the extracted flour streams, the miller obtains a *straight grade flour.* By removing the "worst" 5% portion, or the *second clear flour*, from the flour, the miller produces a *long patent flour*. Most of the flour sold now to large bread bakeries is either a straight or a long patent flour milled from hard wheat. The second clear flour is of low baking quality with relatively high ash and protein levels, and it is "separated" from all grades of patent flour.

In addition to the 5% second clear flour, the approximate separation ratios for extracted flour are as follows:

40-60% Fancy Patent + 35-55% Fancy Clear Flour

60-70% First Patent + 25-35% Fancy Clear Flour

70-80% Short Patent + 15-25% Clear Flour

80-90% Medium Patent + 5-15% Clear Flour

90-95% Long Patent + 0-5% Clear Flour

As the separation of patent flour increases from 40% to 95% of the extracted flour, the ash and the protein contents in the flour increase, too, but the overall quality of the flour tends to decrease slightly. The fancy patent and first patent flours and the corresponding fancy clear flour are not available from hard wheat flour and thus have no significance for the manufacture of bread products.

While the straight and patent flours are used for white and specialty breads and for sweet and puff pastries, the clear flour finds applications in dark and mixed grain breads. Since very few large bakeries still use the better grades of patent flour, clear flour is no longer inexpensive and readily available. Therefore, many bakers now use their regular bread flour with some vital wheat gluten added in place of clear flour.

Whole Wheat Products

There are various types of whole wheat products available to the baker. They differ primarily in their physical shape and how they are manufactured. Since whole wheat contains the wheat germ with higher levels of fat and enzymes, it does not keep as well as white flour. Its shelf-life is limited to a few months, even under ideal conditions. Whole wheat products cannot only become rancid, but their bran portion also acquires a bitter taste which becomes stronger with time.

Whole wheat is available in three different grinds (fine, medium, and coarse), flaked, steel cut, cracked, crushed and stone ground. Because the protein in the coarser varieties of whole wheat is only partially available for gluten formation and most of the protein in the bran portion is incapable of forming gluten, most of the whole wheat products are manufactured from spring wheat with a higher protein level, which can range from 12% to as high as 15% or higher.

Whole Wheat Bread must be, by law, made from only whole wheat products. It cannot contain any white flour. The Standard of Identity for Whole Wheat Bread neither permits, nor prohibits, the use of vital wheat gluten. The use of vital wheat gluten, therefore, falls under the law for *Good Manufacturing Practices*, which states that no ingredient or additive shall be used at amounts greater than necessary to achieve the desired effects.

In contrast to whole wheat bread, regular *Wheat Bread* has no Standard of Identity and may be manufactured with varying amounts of whole wheat products and white flour. The whole wheat products in these types of bread generally range from a low of 20% to a high of 70% of the total flour. Again, the use of vital wheat gluten in wheat breads is governed by Good Manufacturing Practices.

Non-Wheat Flours

Except for rye flour, non-wheat flours are primarily used in multi-grain breads. Since non-wheat flour proteins lack the ability to form a gluten structure, the addition of non-wheat flours to bread doughs usually results in reduced bread volumes, i.e. denser bread, unless vital wheat gluten is added. The Standard of Identity for white bread limits the amount of non-wheat flour that can be legally added to this type of bread to 3% of the total flour weight. However, there are no Standards of Identity for multi-grain and other variety breads. Here, the amount of non-wheat flours that can be added to doughs depends on the specific characteristics imparted by the individual grains with respect to taste, texture, and volume depression, as well as on the cost of the ingredient.

Rye Flour

Even though rye breads are very popular in North and East Europe, they have lost market share in this country. In the quest to produce softer rye bread with more loaf volume, bakers have reformulated their doughs by reducing the amount of rye flour to less than 30% of the total flour weight and by replacing the taste of rye flour with rye flavor. These changes simplified rye bread production, but did little to increase the consumption of rye bread.

Doughs made with more than 50% (f.b.) rye flour are difficult to process and should be baked directly on the oven hearth, rather than in pans or baskets. This requires special skills and equipment, while bread made from 30% (f.b.) or less rye flour can be mixed and processed like wheat bread. The very high level of alpha-amylase in rye flour also makes it necessary to process rye flour doughs at a lower pH level than normally used for wheat bread. The acid of natural or artificial sours inhibits the activity of the amylase and prevents it from breaking down the crumb structure during baking. This breakdown manifests itself as a very dense ("raw") layer at the bottom of rye breads and as large holes below the crust (in severe cases). Rye flour also contains high levels of gums which contribute to the good shelf-life of rye bread.

The milling process for rye flours differs from that for

wheat flours and it requires an even more careful "tempering" of the grist to a moisture level of 14 to 16%. Higher levels of moisture can lead to the "gumming-up" of the milling equipment, while lower moisture levels make it difficult to separate the shattered bran fractions from the flour.

Bakers use several types of rye flour and rye meal. Whole rye meal is usually called *pumpernickel meal* and, like whole wheat, it is available as fine, medium, and coarse ground flour. This rye meal is primarily used for the manufacture of the denser pumpernickel breads. While *medium rye flour* is milled as a straight grade flour, *white rye flour* is lighter in color and is a patent flour with lower fat and ash contents. The name of *dark rye flour* is quite descriptive of its appearance. It represents the portion of flour which has been separated from the white rye flour during the milling process and tends to have the highest ash and fat levels, even higher than the pumpernickel meal.

While light (or *white*) rye flour used at levels up to 20% of the total flour weight (the remaining 80% of the flour weight is clear or high-protein flour) has only a minor volume depressing effect in bread, the effect of an equal amount of medium rye flour or pumpernickel meal is quite significant. Dark rye flour used at this level contributes a good flavor, but has a severe adverse effect on loaf volume. For this reason, dark rye flour should only be used in heavy rye breads baked directly on the oven hearth.

Other Grains

Other non-wheat grains are seldom used at significant levels, i.e., to replace more than 10% of the total flour. Most of these "unconventional" flours are merely ground grains or seeds (reduced to a small particle size), rather than extracted from a plant material. These types of flours are primarily used in multi-grain bakery foods, where none of the various grains and seeds, other than wheat flour, has a dominating effect on the eating quality of the bread.

The following are widely accepted by the public in breads:

Grains
>Oat: flakes and flour, oatbran
>Rye: meal and flour
>Barley: flakes, grits, and flour, malted barley
>Rice: flour and bran
>Triticale (hybrid of wheat and rye)
>Corn: meal and flour
>Millet: flour

Seeds
>Sunflower: kernels
>Flaxseed: whole and milled
>Buckwheat: whole, light and dark flour

The following flours are used in a variety of bakery foods:

Tubers
>Potato
>Tapioca (Cassava)

Legumes
>Soybean: flour
>Peas (green and yellow): flour

Water

Although water is a major ingredient in bakery foods, there is not total agreement on how much "water quality" affects "product quality." This discussion goes back to the early part of this century, when a major baking company wanted to standardize the quality of its bread produced in a number of different locations. When this attempt failed, even though all the bakeries were using ingredients from the same suppliers, it was concluded that the observed differences were due to inconsistencies in "water quality." The chemical analysis of water samples from these bakeries verified that there were significant differences in water hardness, impurities, and pH of the various samples. This finding led to the development of the first *mineral yeast food* by Fleischmann. This dough additive contained the buffering salt calcium sulfate to minimize differences in water hardness and acidity (pH). The salts ammonium sulfate or ammonium chloride were included in this compounded ingredient to stimulate propagation of yeast cells in fermenting sponges and dough, thus contributing to the descriptive name "yeast food."

Although the use of mineral yeast food in bread doughs helped to overcome differences in "water quality," the effect of water on product quality has never been fully answered. In fact, it is suspected that the topic of water quality is often used as "the last excuse" for the inability of bakery production management to solve quality problems in their product. Only in communities with a supply of very soft water or with water having a high degree of alkalinity or acidity may bakeries have to resort to more drastic measures than to merely add mineral yeast food. The manufacturers of bakery ingredients now offer *acid type yeast foods* (containing monocalcium phosphate) for bakers who must use alkaline water and calcium carbonate to buffer very acidic conditions in bread dough.

Yeast

Yeast is a living microorganism and is, therefore, susceptible to injury and even death when subjected to adverse conditions during storage and handling. While the baker uses what is known as baker's yeast (*Saccharomyces cerevisiae*) to leaven his products, the brewer of beer uses *brewer's yeast* and the wine maker uses other specific yeasts in his trade. Not all of these yeasts are suitable for leavening doughs. There are also "wild" yeasts (i.e., yeasts occurring naturally in the environment) everywhere. While some of these wild yeasts may cause food spoilage, others may be useful. Bakers preparing their own spontaneous sours depend on the desirable wild yeast strains. The microbial culture used for the manufacture of the authentic San Francisco Sour Bread contains a very specific yeast (*Saccharomyces exiguus*) which is, unlike baker's yeast, unable to ferment maltose. However, this yeast is able to coexist with the heterofermentative *Lactobacillus sanfrancisco* which produces several different organic acids besides lactic acid, at pH levels as low as 3.8 to 4.5. This special yeast for sour doughs is an excellent producer of the leavening gas carbon dioxide, but it does not tolerate freezing as well as the *lactobacillus* organism and baker's yeast.

Baker's yeast has been produced commercially in Europe for more than 150 years. Pure strains of this yeast, however, did not become available until the late 1800s. What is important to the baker is the yeast's ability to convert fermentable sugars (sucrose, maltose, dextrose, and fructose) into alcohol and the leavening gas carbon dioxide (CO_2). The carbon dioxide is not only useful for expanding the dough structure by inflating air cells formed during mixing within the three-dimensional gluten matrix, but it also dissolves in the dough moisture and forms carbonic acid, which lowers the pH of the dough. Later, in the crumb, the carbonic acid also contributes to the taste of the bread.

While about half of the alcohol formed by the yeast is

lost during the baking process and most of the remaining alcohol is retained in the bread crumb, some of it enters into chemical reactions with organic acids produced by lactic acid bacteria or is oxidized by yeast enzymes into aromatic aldehydes. All these reaction products add to the unique bread flavor.

Even though the baker uses yeast primarily to leaven his bakery foods, baker's yeast (*S. cerevisiae*) is generally not sold in its pure form. It is easily contaminated with lactic acid bacteria during the manufacturing process. George Carlin reported in 1958 (Carlin 1958) at the annual meeting of the American Society of Bakery Engineers (ASBE) that commercial yeast contains one lactic acid bacterium for every five or six yeast cells. However, while the yeast counts in doughs and sponge preferments tended to remain constant over a long period of time at about 200 million cells per gram, the number of lactic acid bacteria decreased from about 12 million per gram in a freshly mixed straight dough, to 6.6 million in the fully fermented dough (2.5 hours after mixing) and further to 3.9 million after four hours of fermentation (overfermented dough). But today's manufacturers of baker's yeast claim to have not more than one bacterium per 100 yeast cells in their commercial products.

Although the presence of lactic acid bacteria in baker's yeast may be the result of contamination, these organisms do fulfill a useful function: hetero-fermentative lactic acid bacteria produce a variety of organic acids which by themselves, or as reaction products with alcohol produced by the yeast, or after undergoing complex chemical reactions during baking, contribute to the delicate flavor of freshly baked bread. The types of organic acids produced in doughs depend on the temperature of the ferment (dough, sponge, or liquid ferment) and the components of the substrate (material or food) the organisms are fermenting. Generally, low temperatures (below 50°F or 10°C) favor the production of more desirable organic acids, while fermentation temperatures of 86°F (30°C) or higher frequently produce off-flavors. Retarded doughs and frozen doughs allowed to defrost slowly in the retarder often produce slightly darker crust colors and small greyish blisters in the crust as the result of bacterial fermentation.

The lack of flavor in bread prepared by the "no-time" dough method, a straight dough processed within 15 minutes after mixing and without having received bulk fermentation, can be explained by the absence of a significant amount of organic acids in the dough. This is because the yeast activity in warmer no-time doughs proceeds more rapidly than the bacterial activity which produces the organic acids in the dough necessary for the formation of flavoring components.

Fresh Yeast

Baker's yeast is available today in several different forms. The most popular kind is the *compressed yeast* (fresh yeast). It contains approximately 70% moisture, 15.5% protein and about 12-14.5% carbohydrates. If properly packaged and stored at 35-45°F (2-7°C), this type of yeast will retain its activity for about two weeks. Even though most bakeries were able to use yeast from different manufacturers interchangeably until the early 1970s, there may be significant differences in yeast performance today, particularly in sweet doughs. These differences are due to the selection of yeast strains and the conditions under which the yeast was grown by the manufacturer. These differences may become very critical in fully automated plants, which do not allow for much variation in proof times.

Compressed yeast is also known in the baking industry as fresh yeast and is available as *crumbled yeast* in bulk packages and as *cake yeast* overwrapped in waxed paper. The cake yeast is now primarily used in smaller baking plants since it comes either in one-pound or in five-pound (five one-pound units packaged as one block) "cakes," or packages, to facilitate the weighing process in these shops. While cake yeast has a fairly good tolerance and can be exposed to the ambient temperature in bakeries for up to 15 minutes, crumbled yeast must be kept refrigerated until it is used. Also, the container of the crumbled product should be kept closed tightly, even during short-term storage, to prevent fresh air from coming into contact with the ingredient. The presence of oxygen causes a rapid deterioration of yeast vitality.

While the crumbled yeast is generally used in a refrigerated water slurry to facilitate metering in automated batching systems such as plastic or liquid ferments, most of the cake yeast is added directly to the mix, either crumbled up or "pasted" with (suspended in) some dough water. This type of yeast is readily incorporated into doughs and starts fermenting sugars immediately, even before the dough is fully mixed.

Cream Yeast

Although compressed yeast is manufactured by concentrating *cream yeast* with a solids content of about 18% to a solids content of approximately 30%, cream yeast has been made available to the baking industry in the United States only since the 1980s. The initial installation of a cream yeast system in a bakery can cost from $200,000 to $500,000 (Anonymous 1993) and is usually amortized with contracted purchases of the ingredient. Stored at the recommended temperature of 36°F (2°C) with slow agitation in the tank, cream yeast has a shelf-life of up to three weeks. It is used for the same applications and at the same solids level as compressed yeast. The recommended exchange ratio is:

1 lb compressed yeast = 1.7 lb cream yeast - 0.7 lb. water

Dry Yeast

Dry yeast is produced by extruding a special strain of compressed yeast through screen-like perforated plates. The strands are broken up, dried to a low moisture, ground, and packaged. Some dry yeasts are also blended with other additives to increase their stability and rehydration rate.

The oldest type of commercial dry yeast is known in the baking industry as *active dry yeast* (ADY). It was developed in the 1940s in response to special needs during World War II. Unless ADY is to be stored for an extended period of time, it does not require refrigeration. If packaged under vacuum or in an inert atmosphere, active dry yeast has a shelf-life of up to two years. Its production combines a special strain of S. *cerevisiae* with specific growth conditions and a carefully controlled drying procedure. ADY has a relatively low protein content (38-42%) and a high level of carbohydrates (39-47%).

For best results, active dry yeast must be rehydrated in warm water before it is added to doughs or preferments. Yeast manufacturers recommend that this be done with four to six parts of 100-110°F (38-43°C) water for every part of ADY. A rehydration time of 5-10 minutes at this temperature is generally adequate.

The reason for rehydrating dried yeast in warm water is that during the drying process the cell membrane of yeast can become very porous. This process is reversed more quickly in warm water than in cooler water which slows down the rehydration process. Cool water may also cause the leaching of up to half of the soluble components in the yeast cell, which include glutathione. Glutathione is a powerful reducing agent which not only reduces the mixing time but also weakens the gluten structure in the dough. This can result in a significant reduction in loaf volume.

On a solids basis, active dry yeast has an activity equivalent to 65-75% fresh yeast. Therefore, for conversion from fresh yeast to ADY, a conversion factor in the range of 0.44-0.5 will give the desired results. This means that a baker should multiply the pounds (or ounces) of compressed or crumbled yeast used in a dough by this factor to calculate the amount of ADY needed to substitute for the fresh yeast. The same result may be obtained by using seven to eight ounces of ADY for every 16 ounces of fresh yeast replaced.

A more stable form of ADY is *protected active dry yeast* (PADY). This type of yeast was developed in the 1960s (Anonymous 1993) as an ingredient for mixes. It has a lower moisture content and has antioxidants and emulsifiers added to it. The emulsifiers facilitate the rehydration of the yeast and thus help to reduce leaching from yeast cells.

The shelf-life of protected active dry yeast can be up to twice as long as that of the regular, unprotected form. Otherwise, there is no significant difference between them. The rehydration procedure and the use-levels are the same for both types of active dry yeast.

Another form of dry yeast was developed in the 1960s. It became known as *instant dry yeast* (IDY). This yeast was the result of a new strain of *S. cerevisiae*, of different growth and drying conditions, and the addition of emulsifiers. It is packaged under vacuum or in an inert atmosphere, and can have a shelf-life of one year at room temperature. Based on solids, its activity ranges from 80-90% of fresh yeast. This means that 16 ounces of fresh yeast can be replaced with 5.5 to 6.5 ounces of IDY, which is a ratio of 0.34 to 0.4 parts of IDY for every 1.0 part of fresh yeast.

Instant dry yeast has a moisture content of approximately 5%. A protein content of 43-44% in conjunction with about 40% carbohydrates not only assures that this dry yeast has a good activity in doughs, but also a very good stability during storage in the unopened package. However, once the package is opened and the instant dry yeast is exposed to oxygen in the air, the yeast's shelf-life is greatly reduced. The unused portion of instant yeast should always be stored under refrigeration and must be used within one week.

It is very important that the IDY is rehydrated either in warm water (86-110°F or 30-43°C) or during the mixing process by its addition to the flour. The very fine particle size of this yeast makes this possible in most doughs. Very dry doughs, such as bagel doughs, however, are an exception and may contain insufficient moisture to rehydrate the yeast during mixing. Regardless of the method of addition used, it is important to remember, that IDY should *never* be added to cold water! The leaching of glutathione from yeast cells during improper rehydration can have a significant weakening effect on the gluten structure. At the same time it also provides the potential benefit of a reduced mixing time for the dough.

In addition to the "regular" yeast varieties, yeast manufacturers also make available special yeasts for specific applications, such as no-sugar doughs, high-sugar doughs, flavoring (inactive yeasts), and others.

Salt

Salt, although mostly thought of as a flavor enhancer, also helps control yeast activity and strengthens the protein matrix which forms the crumb structure of the bakery food. It is, therefore, of utmost importance that the salt is completely dissolved in doughs. Coarse salt, which is sometimes used in underdeveloped countries, should be dissolved in warm water before being added as a dough ingredient.

Since salt affects proteins, it also affects the gluten development in doughs. Even though it strengthens the gluten, it delays its formation during mixing. In order to reduce the total time required to mix a dough, many bakers add the salt after the gluten structure has started to develop. How late the salt can be added to doughs depends not only on how soluble the salt is, but also on how "dry" or "wet" and on how cold the dough is. Salt needs more time to dissolve in a stiff bagel dough than in a soft English muffin dough. With most salt varieties used in bakeries today, two or three minutes of high-speed mixing are usually sufficient for this ingredient to dissolve and to disperse in white pan bread and other soft doughs.

An Alberger natural flake salt crystal. (Photo courtesy of AKZO Nobel Salt, Inc.)

The delayed salt addition method is used primarily in large bakeries with tight production schedules. Small retail shops rarely use this timesaving procedure. In these bakeries, rather than working on a tight time schedule, the baker is generally involved simultaneously in a multitude of production processes so that it is easy for him to forget the late addition of salt.

Although salt is a relatively pure chemical (sodium chloride), it is sold in many different shapes and sizes. Most of the rock salt mined and the solar salt produced by evaporation of sea water is used by the chemical industry for deicing roads, or for water treatment. According to the Salt Institute in 1992, only about five percent of dry salt produced is for human consumption, either directly or indirectly as part of processed foods.

The manufacturing process determines how fast the salt dissolves in doughs. The three major types of salt used by the baking industry are *granulated salt, dendritic salt* and *Alberger salt*. All are produced from heated brine solutions pumped from underground salt deposits. The three types differ primarily in the shape and in the density of the salt crystals formed during the crystallization process.

Granulated salt is available in several grades, ranging from coarse and general purpose salt to flour salt, the type preferred by many bread bakeries. Pulverized salt is also available for almost instantaneous solubility.

Flaked salt, which is also known as compacted salt, is made from granular (cubic) salt that is compressed into flat aggregates with a smooth surface. Because of its relatively large surface area, this type of salt is generally preferred for topping bakery foods, such as pretzels and breadsticks.

The use of dendritic salt in food manufacture is increasing in popularity. In this type of salt, the crystals are modified through the addition of five to 10 parts per million (ppm) sodium ferrocyanide, or *yellow prussiate of soda* (YPS), to the brine. The YPS interferes with the growth of an orderly and tightly packed salt crystal. Wherever the salt crystal incorporates a YPS molecule, a void forms, which increases the crystal's surface area and reduces its density. Both of these changes in the physical structure of the salt crystal enhance its solubility.

Alberger salt is manufactured by a special grainer process. In this process the brine is super-heated under pressure to 290°F (143°C). The pressure is then quickly reduced in a series of steps. This causes moisture to "flash" off and the brine to cool to 226°F (108°C). As the salt crystals are then allowed to grow in open pans, they form a "hopper-shaped" crystal looking like a hollow quadrilateral (four-sided) pyramid with 89% more surface area than a cube-shaped crystal. This extra surface area enhances the solubility of the salt enormously. The Alberger salt is also known as *grainer salt* or *natural flake salt*. The salt is sifted, and as many as seven different mesh sizes are available to the food industry. The unique surface properties of the Alberger salt crystals also give this product very good adherence to food surfaces.

There is also a variety of specialty salt products available to the food industry. Iodized salt was introduced in 1924 and is generally sold directly to the consumer. It has from 0.006 to 0.01% potassium iodide added, which can dissociate over time. The free iodine formed during this process can adversely affect the color of food. This could severely limit the use of iodized salt in commercially prepared products. However, the addition of very small amounts of sodium sulfite or sodium carbonate will stabilize the iodide in the salt and will minimize this problem.

Salt is also used as a carrier for enrichment, such as

vitamins and minerals. This takes advantage of the fact that the amount of salt that can be added to food is self-limiting and lies in the range of 1.5-2.5% of the total flour weight in the formula. Most bakers use salt at the level of 2% of the flour weight. However, not very many bakers are taking advantage of this method to enrich their bread and other bakery foods. Unless the baker is willing to keep two types of salt in inventory, he is forced to enrich all the products he manufactures and to keep their salt levels the same.

Bakers trying to avoid negative effects of this ingredient during mixing or fermentation can resort to *encapsulated salt*. During the encapsulation process, the salt is coated with partially hydrogenated soybean oil at the ratio of 85 parts salt to 15 parts fat. The fat melts during the baking process and releases the salt.

The consumption of high levels of sodium (salt contains 39% sodium) has been linked to hypertension in about 6-10% of the general population. The blood pressure in these "salt sensitive" individuals can be affected (increased or decreased) by the consumption of salt. Therefore, much effort has been spent on the complete or partial replacement of common salt (sodium chloride) with potassium chloride or with a blend of these two chloride salts. One commercially available product is a blend of equal weights of sodium and potassium salt. Both salts have a similar effect on yeast fermentation and dough properties. However, potassium chloride has a bitter and metallic taste, which most flavor panelists reject. Much of this bitterness, however, can be masked with other flavoring ingredients, especially in rich formulations.

Salt is subject to "caking" (lumping) at high relative humidities. Manufacturers, therefore, tend to add anti-caking additives to salt. Besides YPS, calcium silicate, tricalcium phosphate (TCP), and sodium silicoaluminate are used for this purpose.

References

Carlin, G. 1958. The Fundamental Chemistry of Bread Making. American Society of Bakery Engineers, Proceedings.

Anonymous. 1993. How to Evaluate a Cream Yeast System. Gist-brocades, Baking Update.

Anonymous. 1993. Deciding Between Fresh Yeast and Dry Yeast. Gist-brocades, Baking Update.

CHAPTER
FIVE

Secondary Bread Ingredients

Sweeteners

When the baker talks about sweeteners, sugars come first to mind. Even though other sweet-eners will also be discussed in this chapter, sugars play the main role in this category. Most bakers will never use a sweetener which is chemically and nutritionally not a sugar.

Sugars are simple carbohydrates and are divided into two groups:

1. Simple sugars or monosaccharides:
   Dextrose (Glucose)
   Levulose (Fructose)
   Galactose
2. Disaccharides (Composed of two monosaccharides)
   Maltose (Glucose-Glucose)
   Sucrose (Glucose-Fructose)
   Lactose (Glucose-Galactose)

Although the baker applies the term *glucose* primarily to corn syrup, especially to the "regular" 42 DE (**D**extrose **E**quivalence) corn syrup, *glucose* is actually the chemical name of a simple sugar. Another name for glucose is *dex-*

trose, which indicates that a polarized light beam passed through a solution of this sugar is rotated to the right (*dexter* means "right"). Since bakers apply the term *glucose* to corn syrups containing between 18 and 29% water, the term "dextrose" is generally reserved for the dextrose monohydrate (one molecule of water attached to each dextrose molecule), which contains only 9.1% moisture.

Glucose (dextrose) is one of the two sugars in the three most common *disaccharides* listed above (*di* means two and *saccharides* are sugars). Glucose is also the basic building block for the common *polysaccharides* (*poly* means "many") which include starch, glycogen (a starch-like substance found in cells of animals), and cellulose. Since saccharides (sugars) are *carbohydrates*, these polysaccharides are also known as *complex carbohydrates*. While the human digestive system can easily metabolize (extract energy from them) starch and glycogen, it is unable to do the same with cellulose. Indigestible organic compounds are called *fiber*. Some fibers, like natural cellulose, are insoluble in water and are called *insoluble fiber*.

The Food and Drug Administration (FDA) defines "sugar" two different ways. In ingredient statements "sugar" implies regular sugar (sucrose) only. Sweeteners derived from corn or other starchy sources, from milk, and from fruits have to be labeled accordingly as "corn syrup," "lactose," or "concentrated fruit juice." When it comes to nutritional labeling, the Nutrition Labeling and Education Act (NLEA) of 1990 specifies that the chemical and nutritional definition of "sugar" must be used for the declaration of how much "sugar" is contained in one serving of the food. In this particular application, all the different mono- and disaccharides are combined under the generic term of "sugar."

With the exception of the common sugar sucrose, all the

previously listed sugars are *reducing sugars* and are able to "reduce" chemically the cupric ion in a Fehling solution to the insoluble cuprous ion. Under favorable conditions such as dry heat, these reducing sugars react with protein in flour, milk, eggs, and other ingredients, to form the flavors and color in the crust of bakery foods. This "browning reaction" is also known as *Maillard Reaction* and it is a very important contributor to the taste of baked, toasted, and fried foods. Note: There are also other conditions which promote Maillaird reactions.

Sucrose

The two sources for regular sugar, or sucrose, are sugar cane and sugar beets. In the refined form, cane and beet sugar are over 99.5% pure sucrose and can be used interchangeably in all bakery foods. Although both of its components, glucose (dextrose) and fructose, which is also known as *levulose*, are *reducing sugars*, sucrose does not have the ability to chemically "reduce" the cupric ion in the Fehling solution to the insoluble cuprous oxide. Sucrose, therefore, does not react with amino acids during baking to form Maillard (browning) reaction products. Sucrose produces crust color by a different mechanism. It is commonly known as *caramelization* and takes place at slightly higher temperatures than the Maillard reaction by dehydration and polymerization (*condensation*) of the sugar. Caramel color is made by this process.

The enzyme *invertase* in yeast breaks the bond between the two sugar components in sucrose shortly after the yeast comes into contact with the sugar during mixing. Thus, the sugar "sucrose" is replaced in yeast-leavened doughs within a few minutes with dextrose and fructose, which are directly fermented by the *zymase enzyme system* in the yeast. The zymase breaks down (ferments) each monosaccharide component (dextrose and fructose) of the sucrose into two molecules of ethyl alcohol and two molecules of carbon dioxide.

While about half of the alcohol produced by yeast during fermentation is lost during the baking process, some of the remaining alcohol reacts with organic fermentation acids and forms esters which add to the flavor of the baked product.

Although some bakeries still use sucrose in bread production, most large bread bakeries have replaced it with *42% high-fructose corn syrup* (42% HFCS).

Brown sugar is essentially a partially refined cane sugar (sucrose). It contains some residual molasses, which contributes a distinct flavor to the product. This flavor is also the reason why bakers add brown sugar to their dark variety breads, especially the wheat and multi-grain type breads. Application levels are usually between 6-10% of the total flour weight.

Brown sugar contains between 2-5% moisture. For this reason brown sugar is also classified as *soft sugar*. When brown sugar is allowed to dry out, the invert sugar in the molasses residue causes the sugar particles to bind together into a rock-like substance, especially when the sugar is compressed. Once this has happened, it is best to recondition the dried out sugar with about 10% of its weight hot water and slow agitation. This water must be, however, subtracted from other liquids added to the mix.

Brown sugar is available in three major categories: light, medium, and dark. A light brown sugar contains less molasses than a medium or a dark brown sugar and contributes less taste to the bakery food. Some bakers prepare their own medium brown sugar by blending 10 lb. brown sugar molasses with 90 lb. granulated sugar.

At one time, the cane sugar industry graded sugars according to their color on a scale of 1 to 15. Bleached granulated sugar was rated "1" (white) and a very dark brown sugar was given the score of "15" (very dark brown). Light brown sugar would have been called a number 7 or 8 sugar and the dark brown sugar would have fallen into the number range of 11 to 13. Medium brown sugar would have matched a number 9 or 10 sugar.

Brownulated Brand Brown Sugar (Domino Sugar) is a free flowing and pure brown sugar. It will not lump, it is easy to use, and it will produce the same results as regular brown sugar.

Dextrose

Dextrose was first commercially produced in 1921. For many years dextrose was also known as *corn sugar* because it was produced from corn starch. This term, however, is no longer in common use. Dextrose is available in various particle sizes ranging from granular to finely powdered. It is easily differentiated from regular sugar by the much more pronounced negative heat of solution. This is the cooling effect one experiences when one allows this sugar to dissolve on the tongue.

Although an anhydrous (no moisture containing) form of dextrose is available for the pharmaceutical industry, bakeries usually use the monohydrate (one molecule of water associated with every molecule of dextrose), since the monohydrate is more economical to use on an equal solids content basis. However, it must be remembered that this ingredient consists of only 90.9% dextrose solids (fermentable sugar) and 9.1% moisture.

The solubility of dextrose decreases rapidly at temperatures lower than 77°F (25°C), which makes it an ideal topping sugar for bakery foods. The relative sweetness of dextrose is only about 70-80% of the sweetness of sucrose tested under the same conditions.

Dextrose is a reducing sugar. All reducing sugars are chemically more reactive than non-reducing sugars, such as sucrose. Reducing sugars take part in *browning reactions* (Maillard reaction) with amino acids and form the crust color during baking. The Maillard reaction products also contribute the slightly bitter, but pleasant taste found in crusts and in toasted bread. Although this reaction is accelerated by elevated temperatures and a lack of acidity in the product, under favorable conditions it can also take place during "normal" storage. However, the Maillard reaction cannot proceed in an environment of high water activity. It depends on dry heat to lower the crust moisture to a favorable water activity level of less than 0.85 (the water activities of pure water and of bread dough are 1.00 and 0.98 respectively). This explains why steamed and microwaved products do not form a brown crust and why the crumb retains its light color during baking.

Dextrose is completely fermentable. However, when used in large amounts, unfermented dextrose tends to crystallize in the crumb and crust. This manifests itself as "sugar spots" in the crust and in a very firm and dry crumb. Contrary to claims made by some, dextrose is not a humectant in bakery foods! In fact, rather than keeping the crumb of a product moist, by forming the monohydrate, dextrose has a noticeable drying effect when added at significant levels to doughs and batters.

Corn Syrups

There are two major groups of corn syrup available to the baking industry:

        1. Glucose corn syrups (CS).

        2. High-fructose corn syrups (HFCS).

The acid hydrolysis process for the manufacture of glucose syrups was discovered in 1811. (Hydrolysis is composed of *hydro*, which means water, and *lysis*, which means splitting, hence acid hydrolysis implies the breaking down of a starch molecule into smaller components with water and in the presence of an acid). The first production facility in the United States was built in 1831 with a capacity of 30 gallons of syrup per day. After 1873 corn syrups were routinely produced in this country. But it took another 100 years before sufficient quantities of *high fructose corn syrup* (HFCS) became available to the food industry.

As reported by Peter Meyer of PMI Consultants (1990), the market share of corn-derived sweeteners in the United States increased from 1959, when 10% of the 109.8 lb. annual per capita sweetener consumption was derived from corn, to 1989 when 53% of the annual 134.2 lb per capita sweetener consumption was derived from corn-based sweeteners. This represents an increase of about 60 lbs. of corn sweetener per person in this country during this 30 year timespan. The increased use of corn sweeteners in bakeries accounts for a major share of this very significant growth in the corn sweetener industry.

Today corn syrups are no longer manufactured by acid hydrolysis alone. Depending on the desired end product, corn syrups are now produced either with a combination of acid and enzyme hydrolysis or with a combination of different enzymes.

Regular glucose corn syrups are generally characterized by their DE (dextrose equivalence) value. Regular corn starch has a DE equal to zero. On the other hand, when the starch has been fully converted to dextrose, this sugar has a DE of 100. Regular corn syrup (glucose) has a DE of 42. There are also glucose syrups available to the food industry with DEs up to 95. However, even though two syrups may have the same DE, this does not mean that they are alike. Depending on the type of enzymes used for the conversion, a 42 DE glucose syrup may be high or low in maltose. The same is true for the higher DE glucose syrups. Regardless of the composition of the glucose syrups, only the 95 DE corn syrup is economical for use in bread doughs. It must, however, be stored at a temperature above 122°F (50°C), or it will solidify quickly as a monohydrate. Lower DE corn syrups do not contain enough fermentable sugars to be useful in yeast leavened doughs.

Baker's yeast ferments only maltose (disaccharide: dextrose - dextrose), fructose, and dextrose. It is unable to metabolize starch fragments with more than two dextrose units (maltose) in the chain. While 97% of the solids in 95 DE corn syrup are fermentable, only about one third of the solids in 42 DE corn syrup can be utilized by the yeast. This increases to two-thirds of the solids in 62 DE corn syrup. Although these corn syrups are still available to and are used by the baking industry in a variety of bakery foods, only the 95 DE glucose syrup is, to a limited extent, used in the manufacture of yeast-raised bakery foods.

High fructose corn syrup (HFCS) became available to the food industry in the early 1970s. It is manufactured from demineralized 95 DE corn syrup which is passed through immobilized enzyme columns in which the enzyme *isomerase* converts (*isomerizes*) some of the dextrose to fructose. The end product of this process is 42% HFCS. The 42% in this descriptive name signifies that the solids in this syrup are comprised of 42% fructose sugar. The remaining solids are mostly dextrose. Further refining concentrates the fructose content in this syrup to 80 or 90%. The 55% HFCS is produced by blending appropriate amounts of 80 or 90% HFCS concentrate with 42% HFCS. Very little, if any, 55% HFCS is used by the baking industry. Most of it is used by the soft drink industry.

Like the 95 DE corn syrup, the 42% HFCS contains 29% moisture which must be considered as dough water. Whereas the 42% HFCS can be safely stored at 90°F (32°C) with light agitation, the 95 DE corn syrup must be kept at a temperature of 122-127°F (50-53°C) until it is diluted to a lower concentration or until it is added to the mix. While some of the dextrose in HFCS is eventually precipitated from the syrup when it is stored at normal temperatures found in bakeries, the 95 DE corn syrup will solidify at temperatures lower than 118°F (48°C). It is for this reason that most bakeries have discontinued using 95 DE corn syrup in their plants and have switched to 42% HFCS.

Malt

There are two major types of malt on the market, diastatic and non-diastatic. The *diastatic malt* contains diastase, an amylolytic enzyme system. These enzymes are intentionally inactivated by heat in the manufacture of *non-diastatic malt*. Each type of malt is available to the baking industry as a viscous syrup or as a dry powder. There is no limitation to the amount of malt that can be added to bakery foods other than "good manufacturing practices" (GMP) and economics.

Diastatic malt improves the "flow" characteristics of dough, i.e., it helps the dough pieces to spread in the pan. The diastatic enzymes (amylases) in malt break down starch in the dough and convert it to fermentable sugars which are primarily maltose and which can be utilized by the yeast along with the sugars added as part of the malt syrup or powder. The diastatic activity of the enzymes in malt is expressed as degrees Lintner (°L). The higher the °L value, the greater the amylolytic activity of the malt and its ability to break down the starch into fermentable sugar and shorter starch fractions (*dextrins*). This makes diastatic malt an ideal ingredient for yeast-leavened doughs that have no fermentable sugar added. Non-diastatic malts are used solely for flavor and crust color in products in which amylolytic activity is not desired, such as crusty breads, rolls, bagels, and cookies.

Besides the enzymatic activity in diastatic malt, both types of malt contribute the typical malt flavor and reducing sugars for the browning (Maillard) reaction. Malt products also add some color to bakery products. The main benefits are found, however, in the better color and flavor of the crust. Only at very high levels (5% of the flour weight or more) can malt be tasted in the crumb of breads. For this reason, malt is best used in products with high crust to crumb ratios, such as baguettes (French bread), hard rolls, and bagels. There is little benefit derived from the addition of malt to white pan bread doughs. Fungal alpha-amylase will do just as well in this application.

Malt is available in many different forms. *Malt extract* is extracted from malted barley and is offered to the food industry with a diastatic activity ranging from 0 to 400°L, with 20°L and 40°L syrups being the most popular types used in the baking industry. Dry extracts are also available, but only in the non-diastatic form.

Malt syrups are produced by adding corn grits to the barley mash. The enzymes in the barley mash act on the corn grits, and thus produce additional fermentable carbohydrates. There are many different ratios of barley to corn available which affect the price of these ingredients. The enzyme activity of these syrups ranges from 0-60°L. Dried syrups are non-diastatic.

Dry diastatic malts are produced from malted barley flour. Wheat flour and dextrose are added to standardize the malted barley flours to an activity of 20° or 60°L. Diastatic malt powders are recommended strictly for their enzymatic activity and are *not* used to improve the color or the flavor of the crust of baked foods.

Molasses

Food grade molasses is a by-product of cane sugar production. Beet sugar molasses is not used in food products because of its inherent astringent flavor. Most beet sugar molasses is used either as animal feed or as feedstock for yeast production.

After the cane juice is concentrated, the sucrose crystallizes and is removed from the syrup with a centrifuge. This process can be repeated several times. As more and more sugar is extracted from the syrup, the ash content of the molasses increases, the flavor becomes stronger, and its color becomes darker. The baker, therefore, differentiates between light (1.5 to 3% ash), medium (3 to 6% ash), and dark (7% or more ash) molasses.

Cane sugar molasses is classified into four basic grades:

Imported

Mill

Refiners Syrup

Blackstrap

The *imported molasses* originates outside the United States. It has a light and clear color and a delicate cane flavor. Most of it is imported from the West Indies.

Mill molasses is produced from domestically grown sugar cane. It has a harsher flavor and a darker color than the imported molasses.

Refiners syrup is extracted from raw sugar during the refining process. It has a light color and it is sweet. It lacks the true molasses flavor characterizing the imported and the mill molasses.

Blackstrap molasses is the leftover syrup after most of the sucrose has been extracted from it. Although there are some edible "blackstrap" molasses available, these are really only dark molasses. The real blackstrap molasses is used either for animal feed or as feedstock for yeast production.

The baker generally chooses the type of molasses most suitable for his application. Blends of the edible types are also available.

Although liquid molasses contains between 65 and 75% sugar (almost half of it is invert sugar), it is used primarily for adding flavor to dark breads and other food items. Light, medium and dark molasses are also mixed with granulated sugar to produce brown sugar.

Molasses contains between 20-25% moisture. At these moisture levels the water activity of molasses is too low to support microbial organisms, i.e., molasses does not spoil easily. Sometimes sugar refiners add small amounts of sulfur dioxide to molasses to further reduce the potential of a wild yeast fermentation.

Several types of molasses are also available in the dry form. These dry molasses have a residual moisture content of 1.5 to 4% of the total weight.

Honey

Honey is a natural syrup produced by the honey bee from the nectar secreted by flowers. There is no Standard of Identity for honey; but the United States Department of Agriculture (USDA) defines the standards for the various grades of extracted and comb honey. The moisture content for Grade A Honey and Grade B Honey cannot exceed 18.6%, while it can be as high as 20% for Grade C Honey. However, the average moisture content of commercial honey is about 17.1%. At this moisture content, honey has a specific gravity of about 1.42 at 20°C (about 12 lbs per gallon) and a water activity of less than 0.6. Since all unprocessed honeys contain sugar-tolerant yeasts, pasteurization (treatment with heat to destroy microorganisms) is essential for a long shelf-life of this syrup. After pasteurization, the low water activity and a pH generally below 4.5 add to the microbial stability of honey.

About 0.5% of the honey is proteins, amino acids, vitamins, and minerals. Except for the water, the remaining components are carbohydrates, mostly sugars. The approximately 38.5% fructose in honey makes this natural syrup an excellent humectant, especially in cookies. The 31% glucose has a tendency to crystallize during prolonged storage, especially at temperatures below 59°F (15°C). Less than 13% of the honey consists of disaccharides (maltose and sucrose) and trisaccharides or other carbohydrates. This makes honey an excellent source for fermentable sugars.

The organic acids and "source-specific contaminants" in honey give this ingredient its characteristic taste. Elevated storage temperatures and the presence of acids promote the formation of hydroxymethylfurfural (HMF) from simple sugars, such as glucose and fructose. With time the furfurals darken syrups of these sugars and give them a bitter and undesirable taste. However, stored in airtight non-metal containers in a temperature range of 70-80°F (21-27°C), honey will remain in good condition for one year or slightly longer. Non-ideal conditions may reduce this time significantly.

Although most commercial honey sold in North America is from clover fields, the more flavorful honeys come from wild flowers, shrubs, and tree blossoms, such as orange blossoms. Some of these honeys, like from buckwheat, are quite dark and may affect the color of product made from this sweetener. While some of these special honeys demand a higher price and are used only in special applications or directly by the consumer, others may be available at a discount.

Bread bakers use honey primarily to add flavor to their dark variety breads, epecially wheat and whole wheat breads. The honey is added either by itself at levels normally ranging from 6 to 8% (f.b.), or in combination with another fermentable sugar. However, to get any benefit from the flavor of honey in bread, it must be used at a level of at least 4% of the flour weight.

High-Intensity Sweeteners

The family of *high-intensity sweeteners* approved for food use is growing steadily. These sweeteners impart sweetness to the food, but they do not provide fermentable carbohydrates which the yeast can utilize to generate carbon dioxide for leavening doughs. High intensity sweeteners also do not participate in the formation of crust color or flavor. The perception of the sweet taste of bakery foods prepared with these sweeteners is usually delayed until the food is partially chewed. Once the sweetness is perceived it tends to linger, sometimes for minutes after the food is swallowed.

Even though "sugar-free" (no sugars added) bakery foods are possible, their development is not easy if they are to compete with similar product formulated with nutritional sweeteners. Since good quality fresh bread can be formulated without sweeteners and high-intensity sweeteners do not contribute to bread anything but sweetness, they should not be considered for the manufacture of yeast leavened breads.

Fats and Oils

Fats and oils are nature's answer to the need for storing energy in a concentrated form. The only difference between these two groups is their physical state. While fats are solid or plastic at room temperature, oils are liquid. In this discussion of the functionality of fats and oils, the term *fat* applies to all members of both groups, unless stated otherwise. It does not include mineral oil and other petroleum products.

Each gram of fat or oil contains approximately nine calories of energy. This compares to four calories per gram of protein or carbohydrates (starch and sugars).

In bakery foods, fats are used to "shorten" the texture of the crumb, i.e., to reduce the toughness of the crumb and the crust. Fat also tends to soften the crumb, which may then be perceived as "fresher." Fat is an excellent solvent for flavors and thus helps to retain some of these during baking. In sliced breads, the fat or oil in the crumb also helps to lubricate the slicing blades and prevents the build-up of a "gummy" deposit on the blades, which interferes with "clean" slicing.

Until about 1970, most bakeries used lard in bread. Lard was readily available and when the lard was rendered in open vats, rather than by steam, it also contributed a good flavor to the bread. However, meat fats (including lard) were found to contain relatively high levels of cholesterol and large amounts of saturated fatty acids, which are believed to cause a variety of human diseases. Therefore, an effort was made by the baking industry to replace lard and meat fat based shortenings with vegetable fats, which are generally a little more expensive, but usually contain less saturated fatty acids and no cholesterol.

Although bakeries used four to six pounds of shortening, butter, or margarine per 100 lb. flour in bread doughs during the years following World War II, there is hardly a large bakery today using more than three pounds of a vegetable shortening per 100 lb. flour. In fact, most bread bakeries today use only two pounds of soybean oil along with about one half pound of a dough strengthener and an equal amount of monoglycerides for crumb softening.

In addition to their main functions, the high melting point fat-like dough strengtheners and the crumb softeners also replace the hard fat portion formerly supplied by the lard or bread shortening. The hard fat is essential for lubricating the gluten structure for a good extensibility of the dough and also for a good gas retention during the early stages of baking. A non-hydrogenated vegetable oil does not provide these functions efficiently in bread doughs.

The use of two parts of soybean oil per 100 lb. flour in bread doughs is now preferred by large bakeries, because the oil is not only cheaper than partially hydrogenated vegetable shortenings, but it can also be stored in bulk. An added benefit is that the cost for disposing of the packaging material is eliminated. Oil cannot only be metered accurately and automatically, it is also less objectional nutritionally, and it provides significant savings when used in place of three percent hydrogenated vegetable shortening. However, it is not recommended to use a liquid vegetable oil without the addition of some hard fat.

Milk and Milk Replacers

Until the late 1960s, *Nonfat dry milk* (NFDM) was used by bread bakers at the rate of four parts NFDM for every 100 parts of flour. Today, nonfat dry milk is rarely used by commercial bread bakers. Government policies resulted in drastic price increases for NFDM, so that bakers were searching for alternatives. A large assortment of milk replacers was formulated and offered to the baking industry with a variety of claims. While some of these replacers performed well, others soon disappeared from the market.

The majority of milk replacers are based on whey, a cheap by-product of cheese manufacture. Whey supplies the reducing sugar lactose for good crust color development. The addition of soy flour with the whey not only provides the necessary protein for the browning (Maillard) reaction, but also increases the dough water absorption to the same level as NFDM. Many manufacturers of milk replacers, but not all, also formulate this ingredient to contain the same amount of protein (35%) as found in NFDM, to make the replacer nutritionally equivalent to milk solids. However, milk replacers vary significantly in composition, and the majority of them cannot be used interchangeably with another replacer, unless major changes in the ingredient and nutritional statements are made at the same time.

Bakers once added about 4% (f.b.) milk solids to their white pan bread in order to give it good toasting characteristics. Now the average bread baker adds only two pounds of a replacer instead. Although some bakers have also experimented with adding pure sweet whey to their doughs, most of them soon noticed that their doughs absorbed less water and, perhaps, also required more oxidation. Most manufacturers of hamburger buns have discontinued the use of any dairy-derived ingredient without loss in product quality.

There is very little "milk bread" sold today. The standard of identity for milk bread requires that all liquids must either be added as whole milk, or it must contain an equivalent amount of nonfat dry milk plus water and milk fat. Therefore, for a 60% (f.b.) dough water absorption, 8.2 lb. NFDM must be added per 100 lb. flour in the bread formula, along with 3.6-6.8 lb. pure butterfat (4.5-8.5 lb.

butter). No buttermilk, whey, or milk protein can be substituted for milk.

Eggs

Commercial bakers use eggs only in a few specialty breads, most of them of an ethnic origin. Even though many novice bakers believe that liquid whole eggs add moistness to their product, they are very disappointed when they find out that this is not the case. In fact, eggs tend to produce a tough crumb with a dry mouthfeel. To understand this, one only needs to think of hard boiled eggs. Unless one likes the egg flavor and the toughness eggs produce in the crumb structure, the use of eggs in yeast-raised bakery foods should be limited to ethnic breads and to those products which have to support extra weight from heavy fillings and toppings.

Fresh whole eggs are composed of approximately 65% egg white (egg albumen) and 35% yolk. The yolk contains all the fat in the egg (about 10.9% of the edible portion of whole egg or 34.1% of the yolk). Since the lecithin (an emulsifier) and cholesterol (a nutritionally undesirable fatty substance) are concentrated in the fatty part of the egg, these substances are consequently found only in the yolk portion of the egg.

In order to call a product "egg bread" or "egg bun," it must contain at least one medium-sized egg per pound of bread or roll, or 2.56% dried whole eggs in the finished product (about 4 lb. dried whole eggs per 100 lb. flour). The Standard of Identity for egg bread is published in the Food and Drug Administration 21 CFR Part 136.

Fiber Ingredients

Until the late 1960s, dietary fibers were not considered to be essential in the human diet. Dietary fibers are neither a source of energy, nor do they contribute minerals or other micronutrients, such as vitamins, to our diet. Therefore, dietary fibers were ignored by the food industry and the general public. This, however, changed rapidly when two British physicians, Burkitt and Trowell, noticed that people in Africa, who consume a diet high in dietary fiber, are rarely afflicted by some diseases commonly found in the more affluent societies of the western world.

Epidemiological studies and research have shown that an adult should consume 25 to 30 grams of dietary fiber per day. These studies also indicated that the intake of insoluble fiber (wheat bran, cellulose fiber, fiber from oat hulls, etc.) reduces the risk for some cancers, and the consumption of soluble fiber (vegetable gums, pentosans, beta glucan) has a therapeutic effect on such diseases as heart disease and diabetes. Since the mid-1970s, the baking and breakfast cereal industries have responded to these findings by offering to the consumer a wide variety of products with an increased dietary fiber content.

Since most bakers try to combine a high content of dietary fiber in bread with a concurrent reduction in calories, high-fiber bread is mostly advertised as "calorie reduced." In order to make this claim, the baker must reduce the calorie content in his product by at least 25% relative to the reference product, which is the standard product normally available to the consumer. But in order to call a product "light" or "lite" in calories, the baker must reduce the caloric value of this bakery food by at least one third relative to the reference item. A claim of "low calorie" is almost impossible to meet with bakery foods. Such a product cannot contain more than 40 calories per 100 gram portion.

The food formulator is now able to choose from a vast assortment of food-fiber ingredients with varying levels of fiber content. Generally, insoluble fibers can be used at much higher levels in bakery foods than soluble fibers. Refined fiber ingredients are available at fiber concentrations ranging from 75-93%. There are essentially four major groups of fiber ingredients available to the food industry:

Cellulose fiber
    Wood pulp
    Cottonseed lint
Bran fiber
    Wheat bran
    Barley bran
    Corn bran
    Oat bran
    Soy bran
Cell wall material
    Soy fiber
    Pea fiber
    Sugar beet fiber
    Fruit and citrus fibers
Vegetable, microbial, and marine gums
    Seeds: Guar, locust bean
    Tree Exudates: Gum Arabic, karaya, tragacanth
    Microbial: Xanthan, gellan
    Cellulose gums: CMC, MCC
    Marine gums: Alginates, Carrageenan, Agar

While the cellulose fibers, the bran fibers, and most of the cell wall material are composed primarily of insoluble fiber, the gums consist mostly of soluble fiber. Besides the fiber ingredients listed here, there are also others commercially available and used by individual bakers.

Before a baker can choose a fiber ingredient product, a series of questions must first be answered, since many of the commercially available products have limitations to be considered by the formulator. All the questions are important and none can be ignored:

1. Will the baked product be offered as "calorie reduced?" What reference product is available to the consumer? Will any health claim be made?
2. Will the taste, aroma, and color of the fiber ingredient add to or subtract from the quality of the bakery food? Will the particle size of the ingredient have an adverse effect on the texture and appearance of the baked food?
3. What is the dietary fiber concentration in the ingredient? How much extra water will the ingredient absorb? Will the fiber ingredient change the processing conditions?
4. What is the cost of the ingredient versus increased sales volume? Will the new product reduce potential sales of other established products?
5. Is the supply of the fiber ingredient large and secure enough to meet the bakery's needs at all times? Is the availability of the raw material seasonal and limited?

When used at significant levels (5% or more of the flour weight), all fiber ingredients tend to have a detrimental effect on the loaf volume of the bread. The magnitude of this effect varies with the type of fiber ingredient used and with the amount of water that must be added to obtain a pliable bread dough. Experience has shown that fiber ingredients, which absorb not more water than 150% of their own weight, tend to perform better in bread doughs than similar ingredients that absorb significantly more water. To overcome this loss in product volume, bakers usually add vital wheat gluten to their doughs at the level of approximately 0.4±0.1 lb. vital wheat gluten per pound of high-fiber ingredient with 80-95% dietary fiber content.

Besides the loss in volume, abnormally high dough water absorption levels also tend to open the crumb grain and to produce a "tacky" crumb texture, while the extra wheat gluten imparts a slight toughness to the mouthfeel. Some fibrous materials also fail to hydrate properly and give the crust a speckled appearance. Sometimes, but not always, this appearance can be minimized by adding the fiber ingredient to the preferment (sponge) instead of at the dough remix stage.

Of all high-fiber ingredients available, the cellulose fibers are the easiest to incorporate into food products. They are light in color and have neither taste nor odor. At very high levels (over 20% of the total flour weight), however, they leave a dry mouthfeel, which many consumers characterize as "chalky." But overall, cellulose fibers show the least adverse effects in pan bread. An average cellulose fiber length of 35 microns was found to be most functional in bread and other yeast-leavened bakery foods.

The highly refined fibers from corn, peas, and soybeans are used by bakers who prefer not to use cellulose fiber manufactured from wood pulp or lint. These fiber ingredients, however, tend to cause a slightly greater volume loss in bread. Some of these vegetable fibers may even noticeably affect the taste and crumb color of the product.

Unless they are highly concentrated during the manufacturing process, brans are generally not as high in dietary fiber content as the highly refined cell wall material from legumes. Wheat bran has a dietary fiber content of about 42%, while oat bran contains only 16 to 18% fiber.

The popularity of oat bran is primarily due to claims that the water soluble component beta-glucan has a cholesterol lowering effect in human blood serum. However, oat bran must not be confused with oat fiber, which is manufactured from oat hulls and contains no beta-glucan. Because of their relatively low fiber content, cereal brans are generally not suitable for lowering the caloric content of bakery foods to the "reduced" or "lite" level.

Most of the gums, no matter from what source, contain between 70-85% soluble fiber. Despite their high dietary fiber content, gums alone are not suitable for reducing the caloric content of bakery foods. Even though low levels (0.5-1.0% of the flour weight) of water soluble gums may increase the loaf volume of high-fiber bread, higher levels may lead to excessive expansion in the oven, followed by shrinkage, or even total collapse of the baked product during cooling. The film-forming capability of these gums will not allow steam or leavening gases to escape from the product while it is still in the oven, nor will it permit air to enter the crumb pores while the product cools. As the volume of the steam and gases trapped inside the crumb decreases upon cooling, the loaves shrink by pulling the sidewalls towards their center. The shape of the slices cut from this bread then resembles a keyhole, and this phenomenon is called the *keyhole effect*.

High levels of gums change the rheology of doughs, too. The viscosity of the doughs increases so that more water must be added. This extra water makes the doughs difficult to process and the dough pieces become moist and "sticky." Therefore, only small amounts of gums (0.5-1% f.b.) should be added to yeast leavened doughs.

Vital Wheat Gluten

The first patent for vital wheat gluten was granted in 1939 in Australia. Even though this ingredient is now manufactured in the United States, much of it is still imported from Australia, Canada, and Europe. Although all vital wheat glutens have a protein content of 70-76%, the protein quality in wheat gluten can vary significantly with the wheat source and the drying conditions used during manufacture.

After the gluten has been "washed out" from a soft dough, it is dried to a moisture content of 6-8%. The drying conditions must be carefully controlled so that the temperature of the protein is never raised above 140°F (60°C). At higher temperatures, the protein is "denatured," i.e., its ability to form a gluten matrix in a dough during mixing is destroyed (devitalized). The *vitality* of the wheat gluten can be checked by measuring the gluten's ability to "absorb" water. While a *vital wheat gluten* absorbs approximately 1.5-1.8 times its own weight in water, a *devitalized wheat gluten* (heat damaged gluten) absorbs very little water. Many researchers have searched for a simple test to determine the quality of vital wheat gluten. However, other than test-baking under realistic conditions, none of the chemical and physical test methods developed are able to predict the baking characteristics of gluten.

Most bakers using significant amounts of vital wheat gluten in their doughs like to add this ingredient to their preferments, such as plastic sponges or liquid flour ferments. However, in cases where bakers use large quantities of wheat gluten, like in high-fiber breads, or where the gluten in a liquid preferment causes a problem with the heat exchanger, they generally add some of this ingredient (mostly amounts exceeding 5-6% of the total flour weight) at the dough remix stage.

Vital wheat gluten has the tendency to extend the dough mixing time slightly. The added wheat gluten does not seem to hydrate at the same rate as the protein in the flour. Some bakers even observed two distinct dough development peaks in high-fiber bread doughs made with high gluten levels. Although many doughs benefit from slightly longer mixing times, the second peak is not always obvious to the casual observer. It is generally recommended that the baker establish the optimum mixing time for doughs prepared with high levels of vital wheat gluten by "trial and error," i.e., by experimentally increasing and decreasing the amount of mixing.

A shortage of vital wheat gluten in the United States during the mid-1980s produced a great effort to make vital wheat gluten more effective in bread doughs. The Japanese introduced an "enzyme activated wheat gluten," and others found that the performance of this ingredient was significantly enhanced by the addition of 0.5% (f.b.) DATEM (diacetyl tartaric acid esters of monoglycerides).

Vital wheat gluten is also used to increase dough strength, for example, when the product requires a flour with a higher protein content than is available to the baker. Here, every pound of flour replaced with vital wheat gluten will have the effect of making the flour behave as if it has a 0.6-0.7% higher protein content. This conversion factor will take into account a slight loss in the gluten vitality during drying. Thus, to upgrade an 11.5% protein bread flour to a 14% protein flour, one must replace about 4% of the flour with an equal amount of vital wheat gluten. At the same time, the dough water absorption is increased by approximately the same amount. However, when the vital wheat gluten is added to the flour (rather than used to replace part of the flour), 4% of this ingredient increases the dough water absorption by about 6%, or 1.5 lb water for every pound of vital wheat gluten added to the flour.

Vital wheat gluten is usually used when the wheat flour is significantly "diluted" with a non-wheat ingredient or grain, such as a high-fiber product or rye flour. It is also added to strengthen the "hinge" of hamburger buns sold in the retail trade (1-2% of the flour weight), and to improve the volume of whole wheat bread (3-5% of the flour weight).

Dried Fruit

Even though the quality of bread products does not depend on the presence of a fruit, dried fruit can add special quality aspects to bread. Although fruit breads are ideal snacks during the day, most consumers prefer to eat this type of bread at breakfast time. The dried fruits add not only taste, but also fiber to the diet.

While raisins are the most popular dried fruit, dates, apricots, figs, and peels of citrus fruits are also used in specialty breads.

Raisins

Of all the dried fruits available to the food industry, raisins are the most popular variety. Raisins, if properly conditioned with water, provide not only a desirable taste and an attractive appearance, but they also add to the shelf-life of the product.

Thompson Seedless Raisins

About 97% of the California raisins are produced from Thompson seedless grapes. These grapes are harvested in late summer and are dried in the sun to a moisture content of about 12-15%. After processing and grading, the raisins are allowed to equilibrate and to reach a moisture content of about 18%. The raisins are then packaged and protected from drying out. At the ideal storage temperature of 45°F (7°C), raisins will keep for over one year. The low water activity of 0.55 to 0.62 for a moisture range of 15 to 18% protects the raisins from spoilage by microorganisms. Raisins also contain natural inhibitors, such as tartaric and propionic acids, which account for the relatively low pH (degree of acidity) of 3.5-4.0 and which contribute to the long shelf-life of raisin products.

The Thompson seedless raisins are offered to the baking industry in two sizes. Most bakers prefer to use the *Thompson midget raisins* (2,200 to 2,500 berries per pound), because their small size provides for a better distribution of the fruit in the baked product. The *Thompson select raisins* are slightly larger (1,200 to 1,500 berries per pound).

Each size of Thompson seedless raisins is available in three grades. *Grade A* has the highest percentage of matured berries and the lowest number of stems per pound. *Grade C* represents the lowest quality, i.e., raisins with the most defects.

Since raisins have the tendency to cling together when subjected to external pressure, free-flowing raisins were developed by coating the berries with a stable vegetable oil. The amount of oil added to these raisins ranges from 0.5-1.0% of the total weight.

A new type of treated raisin became available in the early 1990s. These raisins are infused with glycerin, which keeps the raisins soft for a long time. Flavors can be added with the glycerin, so that the fruit flavored infused raisins can take the place of various other fruits.

Bleached Raisins

Another variation of the Thompson seedless raisins is *bleached raisins* (golden raisins). These raisins are dipped into a mild caustic solution before they are washed with fresh water. The raisins are then treated with sulfur dioxide for bleaching, followed by mechanical drying.

Zante Currants

Although 97% of all raisins are manufactured from Thompson seedless grapes, the remainder of the raisins are produced from two other grape varieties. The *Zante Currants* are smaller grapes and were, at one time, preferred by bakers. The currants have a much higher count per pound than even midget raisins and thus have a better distribution in bakery products. However, currants are no longer readily available to the food industry. Even though before 1970 Zante Currants were lower priced than midget raisins, their scarcity now demands a premium price. Therefore, bakers use currants today only when the size of the midget raisins interferes with the proper distribution of raisins in the product or with the accurate scaling of the batter or dough.

Muscat Raisins

Another type of raisin rarely found in bakeries today is manufactured from the Muscat grape. *Muscat raisins* are very flavorful and are used in icings and specialty products. These raisins are quite large and they must be "seeded" (seeds removed) in order to make them acceptable to the general public.

Raisin Bread Standard

The Standards of Identity for raisin bread (Food and Drug Administration 21 CFR Ch. I, Part 136.160) requires that "not less than 50 parts by weight of seeded or seedless raisins are used for each 100 parts by weight of flour used."

Conditioning Raisins

Since the water activity of raisins is much lower than that of bread crumb, raisins tend to dry out the bread during and after baking, unless they are properly conditioned by soaking in water. Bakers use many different methods for "soaking" raisins. Some of these methods are good, but some are not very beneficial to the end product. The baker who soaks raisins in excess water and then drains the water not absorbed by the raisins is not only wasting a lot of money, but also discarding the solubles of the raisins which are responsible not only for the sweetness, but also for the distinct taste of this dry fruit. Moreover, this baker has no control over the amount of water added to the dough with the raisins, especially when the baker fails to control the temperature of the water and how long they are soaked.

If the baker insists on "cleaning" the raisins, even though this was done already while they were processed, then it is best to spray or wash the fruit briefly with cold water. A brief exposure to cold water will not cause significant leaching of the raisins. Bakers using this method will allow the raisins to only absorb the water adhering to them. By controlling the temperature of the water and the raisins, the baker can avoid major variations in the amount of water added with the fruit. However, unless the baker scales everything, the amount of water actually added to the dough will be unknown.

Since California raisins have been cleaned during processing, the best way to control the amount of extra water added to the dough is by soaking the raisins in a known amount of water. By adding all the water used for soaking the raisins, there are no losses incurred from leaching the raisins, and dough consistency is assured. A ratio of one part of 80°F (27°C) water for every four parts of raisins (4 ounces water per pound of raisins) always gives good results. This water should be poured over the raisins. When the raisins are leveled in a container and pressed down slightly, the water will reach the surface. After soaking for 30 to 45 minutes, there will still be some excess water in the container, which should be added to the dough with the soaked fruit.

Incorporating Raisins Into Dough

It is most important that the integrity of the raisins be preserved during mixing and processing of the dough. When the raisins have absorbed too much water during the "soaking" process, they tend to break up easily during mixing. But even properly conditioned (plumped) raisins will disintegrate during prolonged mixing. Therefore, raisins should be added to the dough at the very end of the mixing cycle, and they should be incorporated with a minimum amount of mixing. Excessive mixing will not only destroy the integrity of the berries, but it will also cause leaching of soluble components from the raisins. This includes organic acids, such as tartaric and propionic acid, which tend to interfere with yeast activity. Products made from these overmixed doughs will, therefore, require very long proof times and they will lack oven spring (expansion in the oven during the early stages of baking) and volume.

Raisin Juice Concentrate

The same components responsible for interference with yeast activity also act as antimicrobial agents and retard mold growth. This explains, therefore, why raisin bread spoils only under very extreme conditions.

The ability of raisins to retard mold growth has led some bakers to use an extract from raisins, *raisin juice concentrate*, as a natural preservative in bread. However, since this extract imparts a dark brown color to the bread crumb, it is only suitable for use in dark breads.

Raisin juice concentrate retards mold growth slightly, but not quite as well as crushed raisins. It contains about 70% solids (almost all sugar: 70 Brix syrup) and 30% moisture. Both components must be considered as part of the total product formulation. Some bakers claim that the raisin syrup tends to slow down dough development slightly. Also, because of its action on microorganisms, the addition of extra yeast may be necessary.

Raisin Paste

Thompson seedless grapes are also sold as *raisin paste*. This paste consists of ground raisins with no other additives. Very little, if any, of the raisin paste is used in bread products. It is an excellent ingredient for fillings and cookies, especially for cookies with very little or no fat.

Nutmeat

Only very few bread items contain nutmeats. The flavorful English walnut is the most commonly used nut for some specialty breads. In these breads, the walnuts add to the flavor and texture of the bakery food. Pecans and filberts (hazelnuts) are usually not mixed into doughs or batters, unless they are preroasted. Since the relatively mild flavor of filberts and pecans intensifies significantly with roasting, these nutmeats are usually placed on top of product before baking, so they can roast during the baking process.

Peanuts and exotic nutmeats, such as Brazil and macadamia nuts are rarely, if ever, used in bread products.

Spices and Herbs

Spices and herbs are used only in specialty yeast leavened breads, such as stuffing bread and ethnic bakery foods. They generally have no other purpose than to modify the taste in the product. Some bakers also use a blend of spices to color some special doughs.

The spices most commonly used by bakers in breads, particularly in rye breads, are onion and caraway. Garlic and other spices and herbs are used to a lesser extent in stuffing bread and in ethnic products.

Onions are generally used as dehydrated flakes after they have been soaked for about 30 minutes in room temperature water. Sixteen ounces of water for 6 ounces of dehydrated onions (2.5-3 parts of water per part of onion flakes) is a good ratio for conditioning the onions. Dehydrated garlic is usually available as a powder, which can be added directly to food components, often after baking, such as a smear for garlic bread.

Although whole caraway seeds store better than ground seeds, the ground product is much more economical to use. One ounce of ground caraway seed can easily replace the taste contributed by ten to fifteen times as much whole seed. Also, even though the whole seed often adds to the eye appeal of the product, many consumers do not like the whole seeds getting stuck between their teeth. Therefore, the use of whole seeds is generally limited in bread products to the least amount necessary to achieve the desired eye appeal.

Seeds and Toppings

The most commonly used topping seeds for bread products are *sesame* and *poppy seeds*. Both tend to adhere well to the lightly moistened (sticky) surface of proofed and

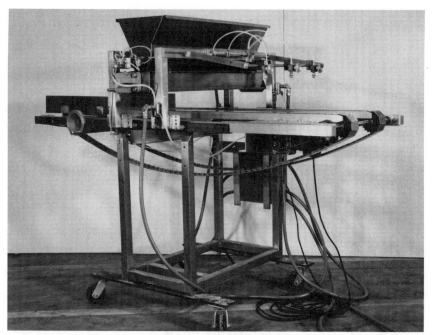

A pattern seeder with spray nozzles. (Photo courtesy of Fedco Systems Co.)

unproofed dough pieces. Also, the flavor of both seeds is improved by toasting during the baking process. Therefore, the incorporation of these seeds into doughs is not recommended, unless they have been roasted (toasted) prior to their addition.

The most commonly used method for applying the topping seeds to the product is by sprinkling the seeds mechanically onto the surface of proofed bakery foods immediately before baking. Proofed products have a larger surface area than unproofed items and will, therefore, pick up more seeds and will reduce the amount of topping lost on pan areas not covered by dough pieces. To increase the adherence of the seeds, the dough pieces are generally lightly sprayed with water before they are passed under the seed applicator.

There are two types of seed applicators used by bakeries. One type produces a continuous curtain of seeds through which the proofed and unbaked product passes. The newer type of seed applicator employs a mandrel (a rotating spindle with grooves in a specific pattern) to restrict the flow of topping seed to only those areas occupied by the product to be topped. This newer type of equipment reduces significantly the amount of waste, i.e., the amount of seed not applied to the product and not recovered from pan surfaces.

Other toppings applied to bread surfaces before baking are wheat bran, coarsely ground grain, flaked wheat, rolled oats, and flour from potatoes, rye, and wheat. Conditioned onions (soaked onions) and whole caraway seeds, too, are used as toppings in some applications.

References

Meyer, P. 1990 (49). Corn Wet Milling. Milling and Baking News. May 22.

21 Code of Federal Regulations. Chapter I, Part 136.130. Standardized Bakery Products. Milk bread, rolls, and buns.

SIX

Minor Ingredients for Bread

Even though this chapter deals with *minor ingredients*, the word "minor" is not meant to imply these ingredients are of a lesser importance for today's breadmaking technology. In fact, all of these ingredients have a significant effect on the general quality of bread products.

Dough Conditioners

The term *dough conditioner* is used by bakers not only for ingredients which truly "condition" the dough, but also for combinations of ingredients with other functions in yeast leavened doughs. Many use the word *dough conditioner* interchangeably with *(mineral) yeast food*. But, according to its descriptive name, the term "dough conditioner" should only be used for ingredients which truly *condition* the dough, i.e., improve dough processing characteristics for a better finished product quality.

Mineral Yeast Food

All "yeast food" contains a buffering salt, which helps to adjust the acidity (pH) in the preferment or dough. While the regular yeast foods are formulated with calcium sulfate, the acidic types contain monocalcium phosphate. The latter type of yeast food is preferred when the water in the bakery is very alkaline or when the baker wants to shorten the natural dough conditioning process, i.e., fermentation.

The true "yeast food" portion of the dough conditioner is the ammonium salt. Ammonium sulfate and ammonium chloride are being used interchangeably for this purpose. When used at the level recommended by the manufacturer, the yeast food will usually contribute about one ounce ammonium salt per 100 lb. flour (0.0625% of the flour weight). The ammonium salt is added to yeast leavened doughs to provide a nitrogen source for the reproduction of yeast cells. It is not required for the fermentation process. Although we no longer depend on the reproduction of yeast cells in bread doughs during the bulk fermentation stage, and the count of yeast cells during this time is generally not increasing, it has been found to be beneficial to the final product quality when a small amount of an ammonium salt is added to the preferment.

Another commonly found component in "mineral yeast food" is an oxidizing agent. This oxidizing agent facilitates the formation of intermolecular disulfide bonds which are necessary for a strong and stable gluten matrix. Most flours produce larger loaves with a better crumb texture when a small amount of one or two oxidizing agents is added to the flour preferment.

Until about 1991, the preferred oxidizing agent in mineral yeast foods was *potassium bromate*. At the recommended level of 0.5% yeast food, this ingredient contributed usually about 14 parts of potassium bromate per million parts of flour (ppm). Today, however, there are many "yeast foods" available to the baking industry, in which the potassium bromate has been replaced with other oxidizing agents (mostly ascorbic acid and/or azodicarbonamide), enzymes, and/or other "bread-improving" ingredients.

Oxidizing Agents

Ascorbic acid is also known as *vitamin C*. However, the vitamin C functionality of ascorbic acid is lost during dough processing and baking. Therefore, ascorbic acid in baked foods cannot be listed or claimed as vitamin C.

Even though potassium bromate, ascorbic acid, and *azodicarbonamide* (ADA) fulfill similar functions in yeast leavened doughs, the mechanisms and speeds of their reaction differ significantly. While the majority of the potassium bromate molecules is simply "reduced" to potassium bromide by giving up oxygen atoms, the azodicarbonamide removes the hydrogen atoms from the sulfhydryl groups (-SH) on wheat protein molecules, so that two sulfide groups can form intermolecular disulfide linkages (-S-S-). The bromate reduction to bromide is rather slow and is accelerated as the pH in the dough decreases and the dough temperature rises in the proof box and during baking. The ADA reaction, however, takes place very quickly and is probably completed shortly after mixing by conversion of the ADA to biurea. Although the added potassium bromate is generally listed in the ingredient statement, azodicarbonamide is considered a processing aid and it is assumed that the finished baked product contains no trace of this additive. Neither the ADA, nor the biurea are known to be a threat to human health.

The ascorbic acid behaves entirely different from potassium bromate and azodicarbonamide in doughs. Ascorbic acid is actually a reducing agent in the absence of air (oxygen). It is, therefore, not a suitable oxidizing agent for "closed systems," such as continuous mixers. However, in conventional mixers operating under atmospheric conditions, enzymes oxidize the ascorbic acid rapidly to dehydroascorbic acid (DHAA), which will then gradually oxidize the sulfhydryl groups in the flour protein by ab-

Protein Molecules

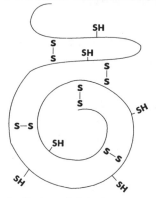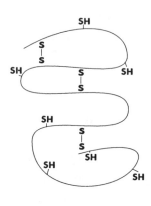

Coiled or folded shapes are stabilized by intra-molecular S-S bonds.

Mixing

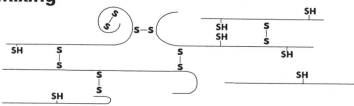

During mixing, intramolecular bonds are physically broken and reformed as intra- and inter-molecular bonds.

Overmixed

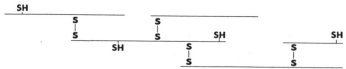

Overmixed doughs contain mosly intermolecular bonds and the dough is very extensible.

Oxidation and Mixing

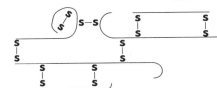

Oxidized dough forms more intermolecular bonds. There are still some intramolecular bonds to provide elasticity to the dough.

Reducing Action and Mixing

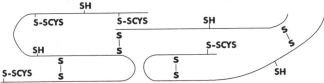

The reducing action of L-Cysteine reduces opportunity of disulfide bonds to reform after mixing action has broken them. This accelerates dough development, but reduces the number of intermolecular bonds.

sorbing the hydrogen atoms from the sulfhydryl (-SH) groups, like the ADA does very rapidly. The rate of reaction of ascorbic acid is slower than that of ADA, but faster than that of potassium bromate.

Another oxidizing agent available to the baking industry is *potassium iodate*. This additive has specific applications and it is not in widespread use. The iodate functions similarly to the bromate, except that the reaction takes place almost immediately after the iodate comes into contact with flour and water. *Calcium iodate* and *calcium bromate*, too, have found specific applications in the United States food industry and are not part of a bakery's "normal" ingredient inventory.

The legal maximum limit for the use of ADA in doughs

in the United States is 45 ppm of the total flour weight, including the ADA added to the flour at the mill. The maximum legal limit for bromates, iodates, and calcium peroxide combined is 75 ppm of the total flour weight. However, the use of potassium bromate in bakery foods is no longer allowed in Australia, Canada, and most European and Asian countries. Use of potassium bromate in the United States is also increasingly restricted.

Because of the differences in their reaction rates, each oxidizing agent functions slightly differently in yeast-leavened doughs. Substituting one for another will often give different results, unless other formula adjustments are also made.

Because the oxidizing agents are used in such small amounts, bakeries usually buy and use them in tablet form. The amount of the specific oxidizing agent added with each tablet per 100 lb flour is generally stated as parts per million parts of flour.

Dough Drying Agent

Calcium dioxide (also known as *calcium peroxide*) is an excellent dough conditioning agent for soft doughs with a high dough water absorption. When used at the level of 27 to 35 parts of calcium dioxide per million parts of flour, it is claimed that up to three pounds of additional water can be added to the dough without causing "stickiness" or difficulties during dough processing. Because this ingredient is used in such small amounts, it is generally sold and used in combination with other ingredients.

Calcium dioxide reacts with other ingredients in the mix as soon as it comes into contact with moisture. This dough drying ingredient must, therefore, be added directly to the mix at the final mixing stage. It must *never* be added with other ingredients in a water slurry, especially not when this slurry contains reducing agents, like L-cysteine, or ascorbic acid.

Reducing Agents

Reducing agents have the opposite effect in doughs as oxidizing agents. Whereas the latter facilitate the formation of intermolecular disulfide linkages (-S-S-), reducing agents interfere with this process. The most frequently used reducing agent in white pan bread is *L-cysteine,* an amino acid. L-cysteine (CYS-H) is the same amino acid which, as a component of gluten proteins, produces the intermolecular bonds between neighboring protein molecules.

Bakers like to use L-cysteine to reduce mixing times and for increasing the extensibility of doughs. However, its use is limited to "no-time" doughs and it is rarely used in sponge or liquid ferment doughs.

The chemical reduction is generally accomplished when one of two exposed sulfide radicals of a broken intramolecular disulfide bond (RS-SR broken by kneading action to form $RS^- + RS^+$) accepts the hydrogen ion H^+ (a *reduction reaction*) from the L-cysteine molecule ($RS^- + H^+ = RSH$), while the remaining part of the cysteine molecule (CYS^-) forms a disulfide bond with the other member of the broken disulfide bond ($RS^+ + CYS^- = CYS\text{-}SR$). By being prevented from reforming intramolecular disulfide bonds (disulfide bonds within the same molecule), the gluten proteins will "develop" more quickly into gluten. But, unless a slow acting oxidizing agent is also added, these chemically reduced doughs tend to be weak in structure and the resulting bread will tend to have a more open grain with a coarse texture. The presence of oxidizing agents will facilitate the reforming of disulfide bonds, but instead of within the same molecule (intramolecular), the new bonds will form primarily between different molecules (intermolecular).

Bakers who do not like to use L-cysteine as an ingredient in their breads may use deactivated dry yeast instead. Dead yeast cells contain the tripeptide (three amino acids bonded together to form a peptide) *glutathione*. While one of the three amino acids is glutamic acid which is also one of the amino acid constituents in wheat gluten, the amino acid in the middle of the tripeptide is L-cysteine. The L-cysteine in this tripeptide is as functional as the L-cysteine added to doughs by itself, i.e., it is a powerful reducing agent and dough relaxer.

Another functional reducing agent is deodorized garlic which is available to the food industry in two different concentrations. If used as recommended, this natural dough conditioner will impart no noticeable garlic taste to the baked product.

Enzymes

Although fungal enzymes are used in bakery products for many different reasons, many bakers add extra enzymes strictly for conditioning their doughs. Generally, enzymes are favored by warmer dough temperatures. Their activity increases by about 40% for every 10°F (5.5°C) increase in dough temperature. However, one must keep in mind that fungal enzymes are rapidly inactivated at temperatures above 150°F (65°C). Enzymes derived from cereal grains are slightly more resistant to heat, even though none of them survive the baking process. Enzymes continue to facilitate specific reactions until they are deactivated either by heat or by changes in the substrate, such as water activity, acidity, reaction products, etc. But most of all, one must keep in mind that enzymatic actions are not reversible!

Application levels for enzymes vary with the magnitude of the desired effect, the temperature of the dough or ferment (substrate), and the length of time the enzymes are allowed to act upon the substrate. While warmer temperatures tend to have a positive effect on enzyme activity, refrigeration inhibits most enzymes.

Amylases

Flour naturally contains an adequate amount of *beta-amylase*. This enzyme splits maltose molecules (two dextrose units combined as a disaccharide) from unbranched segments of damaged starch molecules and thus provides fermentable sugar for the yeast. This enzyme, however, is unable to break down branched portions of the amylopectin in the starch granules. This is accomplished by *alpha-amylase*. This enzyme attacks all starch molecules in broken granules at random places and thus is able to convert even the branched amylopectin into shorter segments (dextrins) for further breakdown by the beta-amylase.

Soluble dextrins (3 to 9 dextrose units) were found to inhibit the firming process in aging bread crumb. Special amylase enzymes are now available to the baking industry as very effective crumb softeners.

Although many bakers buy *malted flour* with a specified amount of alpha-amylase, they may want to add additional *fungal alpha-amylase* to some doughs to provide more "flow" (spread) for the product in the proof box. Others add these enzymes to doughs formulated with very little or no sugar, so that the amylase can produce additional fermentable sugars for the yeast. These sugars also contribute to the crust color of the baked product.

Proteases

Bakers using very tough and strong flours, such as clear and high-protein flours, like to "mellow" the protein with *fungal protease* enzymes, which "cut" the long protein chains of amino acids at random into shorter segments for a more extensible dough. In order to reduce the mixing time of these "tough and strong" flours, the protease enzymes must be added to the preferment since at "normal" dough temperatures these enzymes tend to work on the flour protein rather slowly. In cases where no preferments are used and an immediate reduction in the mixing time is desired, the baker may use a very fast acting protease manufactured from a plant source, such as *papain* or *bromelain*. However, the baker must remember that these enzymes keep working, i.e., breaking down the gluten protein, until the product is almost baked. It is for this reason that most bakers shy away from using these powerful plant enzymes for reducing their dough mixing times.

Lipoxygenases

Another type of enzyme commonly used by the baking industry is the *lipoxygenase* found in enzyme-active soy flour. This enzyme acts on linoleic acid and forms fatty acid hydroperoxides with oxygen absorbed from the air. The resulting reaction product has not only a gluten strengthening effect, which increases the mixing tolerance of the flour, but it also oxidizes (bleaches) the carotenoid pigments in the flour. Some bakers even claim an improved taste in white pan bread made with enzyme-active soy flour, the primary source for lipoxygenase in bakery foods.

The Standards of Identity for white pan bread (21 CFR 136.110) allow the addition of ground dehulled soybeans (with or without oil removed) with enzyme activity of "not more than 0.5 part for each 100 parts by weight of flour used." The addition of approved food ingredients to non-standardized breads and bakery foods is governed by *Good Manufacturing Practices*, which limit the level of their addition to not more than what is necessary to achieve the desired effect.

Dough Strengtheners

As bakers started to use bread flours with lower protein and higher ash contents, the addition of dough strengtheners grew in importance. All these dough strengtheners are classified as *emulsifiers*, although only few emulsifiers are really dough strengtheners. Emulsifiers, or surfactants, are generally defined as agents which reduce the surface tension of two normally immiscible components so that they can form an intimate and stable mixture. The term *surfactant* is applied to substances containing a hydrophilic (water-loving) and a lipophilic (fat-loving) component in their molecule. The lipophilic portion consists usually of a common fatty acid. The hydrophilic component is either a polymer of an ether (polyoxyethylene), a polyalcohol (glycerol), or any other oxygen containing organic component able to form hydrogen bonds with water molecules.

A close examination of the molecular structure of dough strengtheners indicates that dough strengtheners tend to be more hydrophilic than lipophilic, while crumb softeners appear to be more lipophilic than hydrophilic. However, the mechanism of "dough strengthening" is even less well understood than all the factors affecting crumb softness.

The most commonly used dough strengtheners for yeast-leavened doughs are:

Polysorbate 60
Ethoxylated monoglycerides
Succinylated monoglycerides

Calcium stearoyl lactylate

Sodium stearoyl lactylate

Diacetyl tartaric acid esters of monoglycerides

While the polysorbate 60, the ethoxylated monoglycerides (EMG), and the succinylated monoglycerides (SMG) are strictly dough strengtheners, the stearoyl lactylates (CSL and SSL) and the diacetyl tartaric acid esters of monoglycerides (DATEM) have not only dough strengthening characteristics, but they also have a crumb softening effect. Because of the synergistic (enhancing) effect of some of the dough strengthening agents, they are often sold and used as blends with other dough strengtheners in this group.

Although bakers are using the individual dough strengthening ingredients by themselves, they also have available a variety of commercial blends, many of which include crumb softeners. Except for the polysorbate 60, which is a semi-liquid at normal room temperatures, and the ethoxylated monoglycerides, which are soft pastes, all other dough strengtheners and blends of them are sold to the baking industry as dry materials which can be added directly to doughs. The baker must keep in mind that the effectiveness of these ingredients depends on how well they are dispersed in the dough. If, for instance, the stearoyl lactylate is stored in a rather warm warehouse during the hot summer months, it is possible that the particles will soften and compact under physical pressure to form lumps which will not break up and disperse properly during dough mixing. This will then reduce significantly the effectiveness of this ingredient. For this reason, it is very important that the baker follows the manufacturer's instructions for storing dry ingredients. Also, to assure maximum dispersion of these dry ingredients, it is recommended that, whenever possible, they be added to the preferments, i.e., sponges and liquid flour ferments.

Crumb Softeners

There are essentially two types of crumb softeners used by the baking industry: one type is the traditional lipophilic emulsifier, which has been in use for about a half century; the second type, enzymes, has a relatively short history, but an excellent potential.

The lipophilic crumb softeners are generally more difficult to incorporate into doughs than the more hydrophilic dough strengtheners. To make matters worse, the most effective crumb softeners also have high melting points. Although new technologies exist which make the addition of these ingredients to doughs possible in the powdered or granular form, the most efficient way to add them to doughs is either dispersed in fat or as an emulsion (aqueous dispersion).

Emulsifiers used as crumb softeners are of the following types:

Monoglycerides
Diacetyl tartaric acid esters of monoglycerides
Calcium stearoyl lactylate
Sodium stearoyl lactylate

Monoglycerides

Research has shown that monoglycerides of high melting point saturated fatty acids, particularly stearic acid, are more effective crumb softeners than the softer monoglycerides manufactured from unsaturated fats. Because of the difficulty of adding these hard monoglycerides directly to doughs, many ingredient suppliers make them available as emulsions with about three parts of water for every part of monoglyceride. This combination results in a plastic and fat-like paste, which can easily be weighed and added to doughs.

Staling Process

One mechanism by which monoglycerides retard "staling" (firming) of the crumb is relatively simple. But this mechanism does not fully explain the crumb softening effect of the lactylates and diacetyl tartaric acid esters of monoglycerides (DATEM).

The staling process in baked products has been partially explained with *starch retrogradation*. This process is the change of starch in the crumb from an amorphous, random arrangement of starch molecules, to a tightly ordered crystalline state. Like water freezes, and sugar and salt crystallize when saturated solutions are cooled down, the process of starch retrogradation accelerates at lower storage temperatures. This process stops when the starch molecules are "frozen in place" at temperatures below about 5°F (-15°C).

Like many other crystals, starch crystals "bind" (occlude) moisture. Since the starch molecules are tightly packed in the crystal, retrogradated starch (stale crumb) loses its resilience and the product becomes firm. At the same time, as the moisture is occluded in the crystal, the product is perceived not only as "dry," but also as "tasteless," because the occluded moisture also contains the water soluble flavor components in the baked product. Therefore, a stale baked product is not only firm, but also tastes dry and lacks the flavor and aroma of freshly baked goods. Fortunately, the staling process can be at least partially reversed by heating (toasting) the "stale" product. Heat will "melt" the starch crystals and allow them to return to a semi-random arrangement, thus temporarily reversing the staling process.

It has been found that monoglycerides "complex" with starch molecules, i.e., the monoglyceride molecules attach themselves to starch molecules. Since the monoglyceride molecule does not fit into an orderly and tightly packed arrangement of starch molecules in a crystal, it tends to slow down starch retrogradation (staling). There is no indication that other types of chemical crumb softeners use this same mechanism of complexing with starch.

Although there is no longer a legal limit to how much monoglyceride can be added to white pan bread doughs, all other dough strengthening and crumb softening ingredients, other than enzymes, can be used in white pan bread and rolls only at a maximum level of 0.5% of the total flour weight, either alone or in any combination. However, these restrictions do not apply to non-standardized bakery foods, which are governed solely by "Good Manufacturing Practices" (GMP).

Antistaling Enzymes

Much work has been done with bacterial alpha-amylases to control the staling process. The alpha-amylase randomly cuts (hydrolyzes) the bond between two adjacent dextrose units in starch, thus producing smaller segments (dextrins) of the molecule. These smaller sections tend to weaken the otherwise rigid starch crystal. Since the bacterial amylase is usually not totally inactivated during the baking process, a small but significant amount of the enzyme continues to break down the starch in the crumb of the stored product. If this is not properly controlled, the mouthfeel of the product finally becomes "gummy," as more and more of the starch is reduced to shorter and shorter fragments. For this reason, bacterial amylases were never fully accepted by the baking industry. Manufacturers of enzymes have, however, found some very effective bacterial amylases which do not survive the baking process and which keep yeast-leavened products soft and fresh without developing gumminess during prolonged storage.

Preservatives

The term *preservative* is used in many different ways. To some, preservative means that it will prevent any change in eating quality (i.e., staling) or deterioration of product appearance, such as the breakdown of icings and glazes. To most bakers, the function of a preservative is merely to prevent microbial spoilage in general, or mold growth specifically. Since the staling process in bread products and methods to retard it have been discussed, and changes in the appearance of multi-component bakery foods (iced and glazed cakes and rolls) are outside the scope of this book, this discussion will be confined to preventing spoilage of bread products due to mold growth and bacterial spoilage.

In order to properly understand the "problem" of preserving bread, the following important facts must be understood:

1. Bread is free of viable mold and mold spores when it leaves the oven. All mold growth is caused by post-bake contamination with viable mold spores.
2. All agents, chemical or natural, having an adverse effect on mold and other undesirable organisms will also have an adverse effect on yeast and other desirable organisms, i.e., they will slow down the fermentation and proof processes.
3. All preservatives only inhibit (slow down) mold growth. They do not prevent mold growth. The mold-free time period for a bakery product is more influenced by the

extent of the post-bake contamination than by the amount of a preservative added to the dough or batter, i.e., a heavily contaminated loaf of bread will have a very short shelf-life, regardless of the amount of preservative added to the dough.

One immediately recognizes the fact that there is no better "preservative" than the prevention of a post-bake contamination of the product with mold spores. The most critical time for a loaf of bread is the time after it has cooled to about 160°F (70°C) and before it is packaged. Sources of contamination should be carefully avoided. A fan blowing outside air over the cooling bread, especially on a humid day, guarantees a short shelf-life. Flour dust, dirty cooling racks, and dirty hands or gloves can also cause contamination leading to a short shelf life. Common sense and a good sanitation program are the most important preservatives for bakery foods. Chemical preservatives can only lend additional "support" to the effort to slow down mold growth by reducing "opportunities" for contamination with mold spores.

Propionates

Although there is a wide selection of chemical preservatives approved for food application, most of them are not suitable for use in yeast-leavened products because they have a detrimental effect on yeast activity. "Good Manufacturing Practices" (GMP) are the only restriction to their legal use. *Propionic acid* and its calcium salt are the most commonly used preservatives in yeast-leavened products. These chemicals have only a slight inhibiting effect on yeast fermentation when used at the recommended level of 3 to 5 ounces per 100 lb. flour (0.19 to 0.32% f.b.). At higher application levels, propionic acid and *calcium propionate* impart a distinct acid taste to the baked food. Both ingredients are also very effective against spoilage caused by *rope*. Propionates are ideal for yeast-leavened bakery foods since they are most effective at pH levels below 5.5.

Rope is caused by heat resistant spores of the *Bacillus mesentericus* variant *B. subtilis* which is very infectious and causes spoilage of the crumb rather than of the crust. Rope is much more prevalent today than it was during the 1950s and the 1960s. It is most commonly found in moist bread made from stone-ground whole wheat. *Ropy bread* can be detected by its very moist crumb and by the odor of a ripe cantaloupe. This bread disease is named after sticky fine threads which form when a ropy product is pulled apart. These threads become visible when a bright light shines on them.

Sodium Diacetate

Sodium diacetate is another chemical preservative for bread products. Like the propionates, sodium diacetate is most effective in products with a pH of 5.5 or less. Before ingredient labeling became mandatory during the early 1970s, many large bread bakeries used this preservative interchangeably with calcium propionate in the common belief that this change would prevent the adaptation of mold to one particular inhibitor. However, ingredient labeling made it difficult to change from one ingredient to another, and most bakers now use only calcium propionate as a chemical preservative in their bread products.

Sorbic Acid and Potassium Sorbate

Sorbic acid and its salt, potassium sorbate, are not suitable for use in yeast leavened doughs since these inhibitors suppress yeast activity. However, a 5% *potassium sorbate solution* in water can be sprayed on product as it leaves

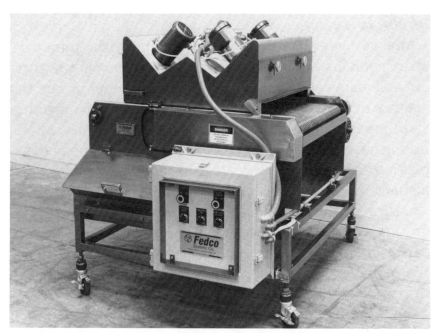

A sorbate spray applicator. (Photo courtesy of FEDCO Systems, Co.)

the oven. This method is quite effective against mold growth, since the preservative is concentrated on the surface of the product, where recontamination with mold spores takes place. Sorbic acid and potassium sorbate are effective at pH levels up to about 6. At higher pH levels the effectiveness of these preservatives decreases significantly.

Vinegar

Next to salt, *vinegar* is probably used more and has been used for a longer time as a preservative than any other food additive. Bakers add up to 1% (f.b.) of a 200 grain (containing 20% acetic acid) vinegar to their bread doughs. However, at this level the vinegar imparts a slight acidic aroma and taste to the bread. Like propionates, vinegar has only a relatively mild inhibiting effect on yeast activity.

Raisin Juice

Anybody who has ever mixed doughs with "plumped" raisins (raisins heavily soaked in water) knows that broken up raisins will not only discolor the dough, but the raisins will also interfere with yeast activity. It is rare that raisin bread spoils because of mold growth. These observations have prompted processors of raisin products to extract a *raisin juice concentrate* (Fagrell 1992) from soaked raisins and some bakers are now using this concentrate as a "natural preservative" in dark variety breads. The inhibiting ingredient in this concentrate is tartaric acid (2% concentration). The raisin juice concentrate also contains about 65% reducing sugar and about 29% moisture. Its natural dark color precludes the concentrate's use in white breads at the recommended level of 2 to 4% of the flour weight.

Fermentation Products

Fermentation products of flour doughs and of whey are another category of natural preservatives. Special bacterial cultures are employed in the manufacture of high concentrations of organic acids capable to inhibit mold growth in baked bread with minimal inhibiting effect on yeast activity before baking. The end products of these two processes are carefully dried, ground into fine flours, and standardized to specified "strengths," i.e., concentration of inhibiting acids. One type of product is offered to the baking industry as a *Natural Dried Cultured Wheat Flour*, while the others are cultured whey products. These whey-derived natural preservatives are usually sold as *milk replacers* and are labeled as *Dry Sweet Whey* and *Cultured Sweet Whey*. Usage levels vary from less than 1% (f.b.) for the cultured wheat flour, to up to 2.5% (f.b.) for the milk replacers.

Even though the active ingredient in cultured whey is propionic acid, these cultured products are not declared as "preservatives."

Labeling of Preservatives

Synthetically produced chemical mold inhibitors in bakery foods must be listed by their "common" name and their intended function must be declared. An example would be: "...calcium propionate (to retard spoilage)..." (Vetter 1993). Ingredients having a natural function as mold inhibitors do not need to be declared as preservatives. Vinegar and cultured whey or flour belong to this category of ingredients.

Modified Atmospheric Packaging

Another method used to control microbial activity on the product surface is to deprive the organisms of a substance vital to their survival. This is done with *modified atmospheric packaging* (MAP). There are two different means to accomplish this:

1. Displacing the air in the package with a mixture of gases, such as nitrogen diluted with 40-60% carbon dioxide. The oxygen level in the modified atmosphere should not exceed 1% of the total gas.
2. Absorption of oxygen in the package by an active material, such as iron filings, which oxidizes rapidly in the presence of moisture in the atmosphere.

These active materials are contained in gas-permeable packets and, if properly sized, reduce the oxygen content in the package to 0.01%. Although not edible, the sachets (sealed pouches) are non-toxic and impart no odor or taste to the product. The "effective life" of the packets is very limited, once they are removed from their protective container.

Another unique way to modify the atmosphere in the package is the use of a sachet filled with micro-encapsulated food-grade alcohol. This system is supposed to not function well for products with a water activity over 0.85. This fact, of course, limits the use of this product to foods with a relatively low vulnerability to mold growth. However, the user of any form of modified atmosphere packaging must not forget that the effectiveness of this preservation measure is only as good as the package itself, i.e., the ability of the film to retain its modified atmosphere and to exclude gases from the external environment.

References

21 Code of Federal Regulations Chapter I, 136.110 (c-12) *Standardized Bakery Products*, Bread, rolls, and buns.

Vetter, J.L. Ph.D., 1993. *Food Labeling*, American Institute of Baking, V-15.

Fagrell, E., *Raisin Usage in Baked Goods*. 1992. Technical Bulletin, American Institute of Baking. XIV(4).

CHAPTER SEVEN

Dough Processing

Experience has shown that the vast majority of quality problems in manufactured goods have their origin in "human error," i.e., in the carelessness of an employee or in a lack of communication. A relatively small number of difficulties can be related to ingredient quality and only very few problems can be traced back to malfunctioning equipment. "Human error" also includes improper scaling and spillage of ingredients, omissions from formulations, and failure to properly adjust or calibrate processing equipment.

Ingredient Scaling

Every step in dough processing can have a serious adverse effect on product quality. Although every step of dough processing can have adverse effects on product quality, the proper scaling of ingredients not only determines that all ingredients are added in correct proportion, but also whether they are fully functional. Ingredients improperly combined during scaling can form lumps which do not break up during the mixing process. This, in turn, can cause non-uniform ingredient distribution in the dough. Ingredient lumps in the bread crumb may also lead to consumer complaints with a potential loss in sales.

Many large automated bakeries have installed automated weighing systems to minimize human error and to increase productivity. However, automated or semi-automated equipment in bakeries performs only as well as the person operating and servicing it. The operator of the equipment must make sure that the holding bins are filled with ingredients specified by the product formulations. The operator must also periodically calibrate the portable scales, while the larger bulk weighing systems and meters must be regularly serviced by authorized and trained personnel.

If the various ingredients are not scaled directly into the mixer or into an ingredient hopper, the receptacle must be large enough to contain the ingredients without potential spillage. On the other hand, ingredient containers should not be larger than necessary, especially when they must be moved and lifted without the benefit of a hoist. Lifting excessive weight can cause accidents and personal injury to the equipment operator. This, in turn, is costly and may lead to unscheduled downtime in the bakery. Also, a properly sized container makes it easier for the operator to verify that the proper amount of ingredient(s) has been scaled. This is especially important for very viscous liquids. A small amount of honey or molasses scaled into a large container may cause too much of these sweeteners to be lost by adherence to the wall of the container.

Small amounts of honey and regular corn syrup, or glucose, are best scaled with other non-lumping ingredients, such as liquid eggs, water, or into a cavity formed in granulated sugar. Ingredients with a high moisture content, like compressed yeast, liquid color and flavoring, should never be scaled into the same container as moisture attracting (hygroscopic) ingredients such as nonfat milk solids, dry whey, or dry malt extract. Hygroscopic ingredients must also be protected from humid air and should be quickly dispersed in other dry ingredients after scaling to prevent crusting and lumping. Crumbled yeast should never be exposed to ambient temperature for more than ten minutes. Compressed and cream yeast are slightly more tolerant, but they, too, should be protected by refrigeration until they are added to the other ingredients just prior to dough mixing. Even instant dry yeast must be protected from warm temperatures and from the oxygen in the atmosphere once the package has been opened. Yeast must never be placed on salt or sugar when it is scaled. If enrichment and oxidants such as potassium bromate, ascorbic acid, or ADA are added directly to doughs in tablet form, the tablets must be broken up and dissolved individually in part of the dough water before they are added to the other ingredients in the mixing bowl.

Dough Mixing

The dough mixing process has three basic objectives: 1) Blending of dough ingredients, 2) Hydration of ingredients, 3) development of gluten structure.

Blending ingredients requires energy in the form of physical action. Although the hydration of flour initially takes some physical action, too, it is primarily dependent on time and temperature. Coarse meals and some fiber ingredients need more time for hydration than fine flours, and cold doughs need more time to absorb the dough water than warmer doughs.

While the blending and hydration of ingredients are usually accomplished within a few minutes, the development of the gluten structure requires significantly more mixing time, i.e., energy input. Bread doughs must be mixed to the point of optimum gluten development. More or less mixing tends to produce bread of inferior quality. It

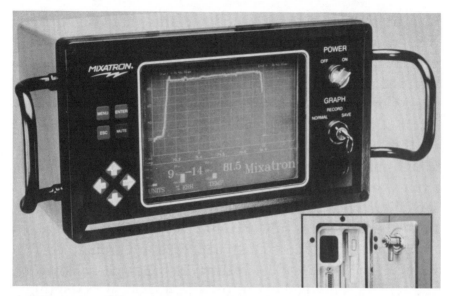

A Mixatron. (Photo courtesy of Breddo Likwifier Division of American Ingredients Co.)

is the responsibility of the mixer operator to determine when the dough has reached the point of "optimum gluten development" and to mix all following doughs equally well. The operator's judgment of dough development is based on past experience gained by stretching a small sample of dough into a thin and transparent film. The operator also considers information received from other equipment operators who report how the dough processes through the automated equipment, and whether the appearance of the finished product is acceptable.

Although the mixer operator is still the person who determines how well the dough must be mixed, much effort has been spent during the past five decades on the development of instrumentation to support the dough mixer's judgment when the point of "optimum gluten development" has been reached. All the instruments, whether they measure electric current or torque, are based on the assumption that wheat gluten is fully developed when the mixer

Plastic sponges in the final stage of fermentation. (Photo courtesy of APV Baker)

has the greatest demand for electric power or the dough reaches maximum viscosity. The requirement for electric power during mixing decreases as the dough starts to "break down," or lose viscosity, with continued mixing. The mixing equipment of the future will have a memory of an "expertly" formulated and mixed dough. A computer will compare current data with information stored in memory and will inform the operator whether the dough needs more water or flour, and when the dough is "fully mixed."

Sponges (preferments) are mixed only to meet the first two objectives of mixing: 1) thorough blending of ingredients and 2) the hydration of flour. The gluten is generally not developed in preferments. In fact, the formation of gluten in liquid sponges is undesirable, since the gluten may separate from the slurry and cause problems by plugging the heat exchanger.

It is also very important that the temperature of the preferment and of the dough is controlled during mixing. The rate of fermentation (yeast activity) depends on the temperature of the ferment. Since preferments are mixed only with a minimum input of energy, their temperature is determined primarily by the temperature of the ingredients. However, gluten development requires a much larger amount of energy input, much of which is absorbed by the dough as heat. Most of this heat is surplus and must be either dissipated or absorbed by other ingredients, such as ice added as part of the ingredient water. Therefore, most of the horizontal bread mixers used in the United States are now equipped with cooling jackets which keep the mixing bowl walls refrigerated. The mixing bowl then absorbs some of the heat from the dough as the dough comes into contact with the refrigerated walls during mixing.

Floor Time

The *floor time* is also known as "bulk fermentation time." This is the time allowed for the mixed dough, temporarily stored in a dough trough or in a container, to ferment "on the floor" under ambient conditions, before it is divided into smaller pieces for make-up into loaves. Depending on the technology used for breadmaking, the floor time may vary from less than ten minutes under ambient conditions, to over three hours in a fermentation room under controlled conditions (82-86°F or 28-30°C with 80% relative humidity). The amount of floor time allowed depends on the following factors:

1. Temperature of the dough.
2. Amount of yeast in the dough.
3. How much of the flour has been prefermented.
4. Level of chemical dough conditioners in dough.
5. Further processing of the dough.

Warmer doughs produce more yeast activity than cooler doughs and thus require less time for the yeast to condition the flour protein during fermentation, i.e., warmer doughs need less floor time. Conversely, cool doughs need more floor time. Unless the floor time is very long (more than 45 minutes) and the doughs are small in size, the ambient conditions have little or no effect on the amount of bulk fermentation required by the dough to produce optimum product quality.

Since fermentation acids produced by the yeast are involved in the conditioning of dough, increased yeast levels will cause the fermentation process to proceed more quickly and less floor time is needed for dough conditioning.

Fermented straight doughs (a dough prepared without the addition of any prefermented flour) require more floor time than doughs made with a significant amount of pre-ferment (liquid or plastic sponge). As a general rule, the more flour has been fermented in the sponge, the less floor time is needed for conditioning the final dough before make-up into loaves. While a 78°F (25.5°C) dough prepared from a plastic sponge in which 80% of the flour has been prefermented will be given only about ten minutes floor time, a similar dough utilizing a liquid sponge with 30% of the total flour prefermented may require a floor time of 45 minutes.

The floor time for regular straight doughs depends on the yeast level in the dough and on the dough tempera-ture. A 77°F (25°C) straight dough with 2.5% (f.b.) yeast may need three hours or more bulk fermentation time when the entire dough is fermented as one unit or "in bulk." Rais-ing the dough temperature to 81°F (27°C) and the yeast level to 3% of the flour weight reduces the needed floor time by about half, to about 1.5 hours.

No-time doughs are straight doughs, too. However, these doughs are conditioned by the addition of chemicals rather than by fermentation. L-cysteine, a reducing agent, is nor-mally added to no-time doughs at the level of about 30 parts per million (f.b.) to facilitate dough development (reduce the mixing time), and to "mellow" the gluten structure. However, most dough conditioning in no-time doughs is accomplished by oxidizing agents, such as potassium bro-mate (25 to 45 ppm f.b.) or ascorbic acid (60 to 120 ppm). Until recently, potassium bromate was usually the oxidant of choice by manufacturers using the no-time dough method. Azodicarbonamide (ADA) is a fast-acting oxidant and should not be added with L-cysteine, since these two dough conditioning agents could react with each other, rather than acting separately on the flour protein. The need for oxidizing agents is significantly greater in no-time doughs than in regular straight doughs, which are subjected to a bulk fermentation period.

No-time straight doughs are usually mixed to a temperature of 82°F (28°C) or slightly warmer. Together with a compressed yeast level of 3% (f.b.) or slightly higher, these doughs tend to be quite active soon after mixing.

In contrast to regular no-time straight doughs, frozen doughs contain even higher compressed yeast levels and are mixed to a temperature of less than 68°F (20°C) to minimize yeast activity before freezing. To keep this activity at a minimum, doughs destined for the freezer are not only kept cool, but they are also processed without delay into loaves and are given no floor time for bulk fermentation. Research has indicated that yeast cells activated for fermentation will not tolerate the freezing process as well as fresh yeast cells which have remained dormant since they were originally produced.

Dividing and Rounding

In order to obtain constant scaling weights with a dough divider measuring dough volume rather than weight, the dough must be well degassed. This is especially important for doughs with long bulk fermentation times after mixing, such as regular straight doughs. Degassing of doughs is generally achieved with pumps "bleeding" the gas from the dough and venting it to the environment. If this cannot be done, the divider operator must constantly check the dough scaling weight and make the necessary adjustments in the volume of dough needed to meet the specified scaling weight for the particular product. It is also very important for a uniform scaling weight that the amount of dough feeding into the divider hopper remains as constant as possible.

The dough scaling weight is usually about 10% greater

than the desired product net weight. Most states in the United States require that the bread weights are in four ounce increments, i.e., 12 oz, 16 oz (1 lb.), 20 oz (1 1/4 lb.), 24 oz (1 1/2 lb.), etc. This means that the scaling weight for a 20 oz loaf should be about 22 oz dough per loaf. However, many bakeries use higher scaling weights, not because their bake-out loss is more than 10%, but because their divider is not "scaling" the dough accurately enough and the bakery management is afraid of being accused of selling under-weight bread. Variances from the "theoretical" and ideal dough weight obtained with a pocket divider are often caused by one of the following factors:

1. Equipment wear.
2. Failure to calibrate all divider pistons.
3. Incorrect viscosity of divider oil.
4. Fear of the operator to produce underweight bread.

A reciprocating pocket divider has many moving parts, which eventually show wear. Since the pistons suck the dough into the "pockets" by vacuum, wear on the pistons or on the cut-off blade can cause a partial loss of the vacuum and the dough weight becomes inconsistent from cut to cut.

Most pocket dividers have more than one pocket. If the pistons for the pockets are not properly adjusted to yield the same amount of dough with every cut for all pockets, the operator is forced to adjust the common setting for all divider pockets in such a way that even the smallest pocket will yield the full scaling weight of dough. Such constant over-adjustments of the remaining pockets can lead to a tremendous amount of waste and consequent loss of profit.

It is very important that the divider operator uses a divider oil with the proper viscosity. The divider oil is a highly refined food grade mineral oil. The equipment manufacturer generally recommends the use of a relatively low viscosity oil. The purpose of the oil is not only to lubricate the machine parts coming into contact with dough, but also to improve the vacuum when the piston retracts and literally "sucks" the dough into the pocket of the divider. However, as the parts in the divider show wear with time, a low viscosity oil may no longer be able to seal the gaps between the machine parts efficiently and the scaling weights for the dough show larger and larger variations. Sometimes, but not always, a higher viscosity mineral oil will temporarily reduce the variation in the scaling weight. However, one must keep in mind that the oil viscosity also affects the spreading of the oil and, in the long run, this temporary "solution" may lead to increased wear in the mechanism and to a major overhaul of the equipment.

Bakery workers are usually not trained in statistics and have no understanding of the normal (natural) distribution curve (also known as "bell-shaped curve") for measurements of any kind. Therefore, in order to avoid an occasional under-weight dough piece, a conscientious equipment operator tends to overscale all dough pieces, especially if the bakery has ever been cited for underweight product in the market place. A divider operator should, therefore, be instructed that it is "normal" for an occasional dough piece to be either very light or very heavy. This phenomenon is a characteristic of all equipment and is independent of the weight setting. How much deviation from the scaling weight and how often very high and low weights are experienced depends on the mechanical condition of the equipment. In any case, a poorly maintained divider is not only frustrating for the operator, but it is also a money loser for the bakery!

Although a mechanical rounder is an important piece of

dough processing equipment, it does not require much service during operation, other than that the flour duster is turned on and kept filled with flour. While "dry," or stiff, doughs need very little dusting flour, soft and wet doughs need a considerable amount to prevent sticking or doubling up (fusion of two dough pieces).

Intermediate Proof

After dividing and rounding, the dough pieces are allowed to "relax" for a few minutes to recover their extensibility for further processing. The time allowed for *intermediate proofing* is generally in the range of 5-15 minutes. During this time, the rounded dough pieces move on cloth-covered trays through a cabinet-like enclosure, which protects the dough from drying and forming a crust. This enclosure is usually mounted above other equipment and it is, therefore, generally referred to as the *overhead proofer*.

Soft and "relaxed" doughs require less intermediate proof time than stiff doughs lacking extensibility. While "soft" white bread dough pieces at 80°F (27°C) may need only 5 to 7 minutes to relax (proof) for further processing, 78°F (25.5°C) dough pieces for French bread may require 15 minutes intermediate proof time before moulding into elongated loaves.

In most bakeries, overhead proofers are operated under ambient conditions, i.e. they are neither heated, nor controlled for humidity. Unless there is dry air flowing through the proofer, the relatively short residence time of the dough pieces in the proofer is insufficient for the formation of a dry crust on the dough pieces. The introduction of extra humidity into the intermediate proofer is, in most bakeries, not advisable. An appreciable humidity level may lead not only to mold growth on the cloth trays, but it may also cause the dough pieces to not release properly from the trays.

Bread Moulding and Panning

Mechanical bread moulding, i.e., forming of a loaf from the rounded dough piece, is very similar to the hand moulding procedure used by a baker. This involves four steps:

1. Flattening and degassing of the dough piece.
2. Curling (rolling up) of dough into a cylinder.
3. Moulding and fusing the dough layers together.
4. Panning of formed dough piece.

Each of these steps is performed by a different section of the automatic moulder/panner. The flattening and degassing of the dough piece is accomplished with two or three sets of rollers with a smooth surface which compress and elongate, or sheet, the dough piece. During this process, gas bubbles in the dough are "squeezed" out. Thus, the dough piece is *degassed*. Although tight settings with a narrow gap between the sheeting rollers are more efficient for degassing, the gap should not be so tight that gas cells are ruptured and the skin of the dough piece is broken. This can lead to a very poor crumb texture and structure.

During the next step, the flattened dough piece is moved by a conveyor belt under a *curling chain*. This "chain" consists of metal rods or heavy wires a little longer than the dough pieces are wide. These rods are parallel to each other and connected at the ends in such a way that the chain can "flex" as the dough piece passes under it. As the flat dough piece first touches the chain, the leading edge of it is "flipped" up, folded over, and held back by the curling chain. This causes the entire flattened dough piece to curl up and to assume a cylindrical shape. How tightly the dough is curled depends on the weight and length of the curling chain. At this point, the individual curls of the dough cylinder are generally not sealed together, and they can easily be separated from one another. This, however, is taken care of in the next step.

After the rolled-up dough cylinder emerges from the curling chain, the conveyer belt carries it to the *pressure board*. The pressure board is mounted above the conveyor belt and the amount of clearance between the board and the belt can be adjusted according to the size and the make-up characteristics of the dough piece. The pressure board is usually padded and also covered with a movable canvas belt to facilitate clean-up whenever dough pieces get stuck under it. The clearance between the conveyor belt and the pressure board is usually slightly greater at the entrance point than at the exit. There should be enough pressure on the dough piece to fuse the individual dough curls together, but not so much pressure, that the loaf is elongated or "deformed" into a dumbbell where the ends are thicker than the middle. Too much pressure can also cause the loss of "shavings" from the loaf ends when the dough is forced against the guides which seal the ends and determine the length of the moulded loaf. Tightening the pressure board will not correct textural problems in the baked bread caused by improper sheeting and degassing. In fact, pressure boards adjusted too tightly tend to create their own textural problems in baked bread or they aggravate those created by other causes.

Cross-sheeting moulders require a very relaxed and soft dough, which is well degassed. Since the dough piece changes its direction by 90 degrees between degassing and curling, conveyor speeds and the position of the deflector-plate on the moulding table are quite critical. If the dough is too stiff, or the conveyor belt speed on the sheeter table is not adjusted properly, the moulded dough pieces may be misshaped.

Tendercurl moulders require an even more relaxed dough piece for the proper elongation of the curled dough piece prior to the final curl which gives the bread the appearance of a twisted loaf. In order to achieve the necessary elongation, the pressure board on tendercurl moulders is generally a little wider than normal pressure boards. After elongation to about 20 inches (50 centimeters), the moulded dough piece is picked up by a "transfer" belt which deposits the loaf onto the tendercurl table at an angle of about 30° to the direction of the conveyor belt. The tendercurl table itself is located at a right (90°) angle to the moulding table. After the elongated dough cylinder is deposited at an angle onto the conveyor belt of the curling table, the leading end of the moulded piece is slightly flattened before the curling chain transforms the long dough piece into a tightly curled loaf.

The moulded and shaped loaves are then dropped automatically into baking pans, transported by a heavy-duty pan conveyor below the moulding or curling table. A panstop holds the pans in position until a micro switch is triggered by the loaf before it drops into the pan. The filled pan is then released by the pan stop and is replaced with a new pan which, again, is temporarily held in place by the pan stop. Short chains and pan guides are used to make sure that each loaf is placed into its pan in the proper position and with the "seam" (trailing edge of the moulded dough piece) facing down.

Final Proof

The pans with the freshly moulded loaves are then placed into, or conveyed through, the proof box. The residence time for the loaves in the final proofer is generally about one hour. This time is usually regulated by the baker with the amount of yeast added to the dough. While, however, some bakers of no-time dough hearth-baked bread prefer slightly shorter proof times, producers of sour dough bread must often contend with much longer times at lower proof temperatures.

Loaves made from no-time doughs usually contain more yeast and tend to be warmer than those made from preferments or straight doughs. These two conditions lead to increased yeast activity and reduced proof times. On the other hand, bacteria in sour dough cultures compete with yeast for fermentable sugars and thus interfere with yeast activity. Also, many organic acids produced by bacteria have an inhibiting effect on baker's yeast, while acid-tolerant wild yeast strains are often slow gas producers and may not be present in sufficient numbers for sour dough loaves to proof at the same rate as regular pan bread.

While European bakers are cautioned against using proof temperatures over 104°F (40°C), American bakeries prefer to operate their proof boxes at temperatures ranging from 108-115°F (42-46°C) with a relative humidity of 80-85%. This represents a differential of 5-6°F (3-3.5°C) between dry and wet bulb thermometers. The surface of the loaves in the proof box should neither be wet and tacky (sticky), nor very dry and crusty. "Wet" dough surfaces may not produce a uniform crust color, while a dry crust will cause the baked product to have a top crust with a "raspy," rough feel to it. Dry crusts lack the characteristic light sheen or gloss produced by starch gelatinization during baking generally referred to as "bloom."

Bakers use two different methods for measuring the amount of final fermentation, or "proof," they want to give their product before baking. Both methods are based on prior experience, i.e., previously obtained results under similar circumstances. The first method is based on the size of the proofed product. Here the baker simply estimates the amount of expansion of the dough piece by comparing its height to a reference, usually the height of the pan in which it is to be baked. Some bakers also use a template, a simple mechanical device, for measuring the expansion or height of the proofed loaf. When the product is placed on a flat surface and the use of a template is not practical or possible, the baker determines the amount of proof a product has received by simply touching it carefully and judging the dough's resistance to pressure or deformation. The feel of the dough changes gradually as it expands during proofing. It changes from "tight" and "firm" (little or no proof) to "slightly soft" (short proof) and "soft," but still exhibiting resilience, i.e., leaving no permanent depression when touched which indicates full proof. When the dough feels "very soft" and leaves a permanent depression in the dough piece where touched with a finger, the product is over-proofed. The proofed loaf should not collapse when it is jarred in the pan, when it is cut with a knife or water jet, or when it is transferred from a proofing tray to the baking hearth.

Baking

Bakers are no longer interested in producing "the largest loaf of bread in town." Instead, bakers are very much interested in producing loaves of the same size and appearance from day to day and throughout the entire year. Bread loaves significantly larger or smaller than the "standard size" for the bakery will not properly fit into the bread bags and may thus be considered unsaleable rejects. For this reason, most bakers proof their bread to almost full size and then restrict the expansion of the loaves in the oven by baking the bread with as high a heat as possible. This method also has the advantage that the thin crust formed by intensive heat (450°F or 232°C) will interfere with the loss of moisture through evaporation during the baking process, and it will thus "seal in" the moisture during baking. As a general rule, a short and high-temperature bake will not only restrict loaf expansion during baking, but it will also reduce the loss of moisture from the product. If, however, maximum loaf volume is desired, then the bread should be baked at a lower temperature to allow more gas production by the yeast during the early stages of baking and before the yeast cells are inactivated by the increasing temperature.

Bread is baked when the internal crumb temperature reaches about 201°F (94°C). Continued baking will only cause the bread to dry out and lose shelf-life. Internal crumb temperature during continued baking will gradually climb to the boiling point of pure water, i.e., to 212°F (100°C) at sea level elevation.

Research done at the American Institute of Baking (AIB) indicates that overbaking of bread causes a significant increase in crumb firmness (higher numbers indicate a firmer crumb structure) of bread loaves stored for seven days at 77°F (25°C).

Crumb Firmness of Bread
(1 lb. loaves made by sponge-dough method)

Baking Time (Minutes)	Crumb Firmness (Grams of Force) Days After Baking		
	1 Day	3 Days	7 Days
18	157	268	397
21	188	278	429
24	197	310	461

The effect of overbaking on the shelf-life of bread in terms of crumb firmness equals approximately one day of shelf-life for every three minutes of extra baking time. Moreover, overbaked bread is also much drier and will, therefore, lack flavor.

Hearth breads are baked without pans and directly on the oven hearth (heated surface in the oven). Since these breads have no physical constraints, the doughs are generally stiff and "dry" and the loaves are proofed at a relatively low relative humidity to facilitate cutting across the top surface and transferring the loaves to the oven hearth. This causes the crust to look dull (lack "bloom") after baking. This problem with the appearance of the bread can be avoided by filling the oven chamber with "wet" (low pressure) steam for the first three to five minutes of baking time. The steam literally "cooks" the starch on the crust surface and gelatinizes it. This very thin layer of gelatinized starch gives a slight gloss to the crust, which the baker calls "bloom."

Steam keeps the crust forming on the loaves extensible for slightly longer during baking. It also causes the heat to penetrate more rapidly into the dough, thus killing the yeast a little sooner. Both of these effects are useful for controlling "bursting" (formation of wild breaks near the bottom of loaves) of the bread in the oven.

When a loaf of pan bread is fully baked, it shrinks and starts to pull away from the pan wall. It is not as easy to determine when a loaf baked on the oven hearth has reached the proper internal temperature. An experienced baker will knock on the bottom crust of the loaves. By listening to the "hollow" sound the crust makes, the baker can tell when the bread is properly baked.

Cooling

As mentioned earlier in this book, it is very important that baked products are properly cooled under controlled conditions. During the cooling stage, the bread crumb is allowed to become sufficiently firm through retrogradation or crystallization of the amylose fraction of the starch so that the bread can be sliced and the loaves will not collapse during handling. However, uncontrolled cooling of the product can seriously reduce the product's shelf-life through:

1. Dehydration of the crust and crumb.
2. Potential contamination with mold spores.

Cooling baked foods in a dry environment will cause excessive moisture loss and an accelerated cooling rate. While under normal conditions the cooling rate may have a slight, but negligible effect on staling, an excessive moisture loss may accentuate the dry mouthfeel of the product when it stales. Bakeries may, therefore, want to adjust the cooling time for their breads to the varying seasonal conditions, e.g., shorter cooling times during the winter months, when the relative humidity in the bakery tends to be low.

The mold-free shelf-life of bakery foods is not determined by the amount of chemical or "natural" preservatives added to doughs, but by the amount of contamination the product receives during the cooling phase. The water activity of the product, too, is an important factor, e.g., a dry product will not support mold growth as readily as a moist one. However, unless the product is contaminated with a heavy dose of mold spores during the cooling stage, no mold will grow on it, regardless of existing favorable conditions. Sanitary cooling conditions are the best guarantee for a mold-free shelf-life of baked foods!

Bread Formulations

Upscaling and Downscaling Formulations

The formulations in this chapter can easily be *upscaled* to yield larger batches by multiplying the quantities listed under "baker's percent" by a factor that yields the desired total amount. If the total amount in the "baker's percent" column is 183% and a 365 lb.. (or kilogram) dough is needed, simply multiply all the numbers in this column by a factor of "2" (2 times 183 lb. = 366 lb.). This method can be used for upscaling and downscaling batch sizes regardless of the type of weight measuring unit (ounce, pound, gram, kilogram, etc.) used at the bakery. The formulations offered in this chapter in pounds and ounces represent a direct conversion of the "baker's percent" to ounces, i.e., lb. and oz. (6 lb. 4 oz. flour = 100 oz. flour).

There is no uniform rule in the baking industry for what should be included in the total flour weight. The formulas in this chapter include in the total flour weight, vital wheat gluten, other wheat products, rye products, all grains and seeds incorporated into multigrain bread doughs, and high-fiber ingredients.

Conversion of Bread Making Procedure

Most breads can be prepared by any method described earlier in this book. If ingredients, like some coarse grains and fiber ingredients, require a longer hydration time than afforded in a no-time straight dough, these ingredients can be presoaked in part of the dough water. There are some basic rules to follow when one converts from a "sponge and dough" method to a to no-time straight dough:

1. Increase dough water absorption by 2 to 4% f.b.
2. Increase compressed yeast by 1% f.b.
3. Increase mixing time
4. Increase dough temperature to 82°F (28°C)

The opposite adjustments become necessary for converting a no-time straight dough to a dough utilizing a preferment.

Although the formulations offered in this chapter are all functional, they may require minor adjustments for optimization. These adjustments become necessary because of the variability of flour from various mills and from year to year. These include minor changes in dough water absorption and oxidation (ascorbic acid) requirements.

Ingredient Substitution

A baker may also want to replace nonfat dry milk with a suitable replacer. Granulated sugar may be used in place of 42% high fructose corn syrup. This change, however, must take into account that this corn syrup contains 29% moisture.

For convenience and other good reasons, many bakers now use the dry forms of egg products, milk, honey, molasses, malt, and caramel color. In most cases the quality of the finished product is not significantly affected by switching from liquid to dry ingredients, provided the conversion is done properly and according to the recommendations of the ingredient supplier. In some cases, however, the taste and texture of the product may be altered slightly. Therefore, a baker contemplating such a change must carefully evaluate the eating quality of products prepared with the new dry ingredients.

Since mixers, proof box conditions, and ovens vary considerably from bakery to bakery, no detailed instructions can be offered for these processes. Under less than ideal conditions for fermentation and proofing, the yeast level may have to be adjusted slightly from season to season and to suit production schedules. Convection ovens, which include rack ovens, develop a more intense heat at the same temperature. The optimum baking temperature in these forced air ovens is, therefore, usually about 30-36°F (17-20°C) lower than in regular gas ovens.

White Pan Bread

It is difficult to say whether white pan bread helped form the eating habits of the citizens on the North American continent, or whether the preferences and lifestyle of these people caused the evolution of this popular bread, which still holds the largest market share of all bread sold in the United States and in Canada. Lahvic (1992) said more than 54.5% of total bread produced in the United States during 1992 was of this type. In 1992 white pan bread represented a market of about $3.6 billion in the United States alone (Lahvic and Malovanic 1992).

The appeal of white pan bread to the consumer and baker is based on the following product qualities:

1. Manufactured from 100% wheat flour.
2. Tender and soft texture.

3. Attractive light crumb color.
4. Flavor and taste compatible with other foods.
5. Pre-sliced for consumption.
6. Good toasting properties.
7. Good keeping quality in original package.
8. Good nutritional value.
9. Economical.
10. Easy to manufacture and to distribute.

The composition of white pan bread in the United States is defined by 21 CFR Chapter I, Part 136. This regulation limits the amount of total moisture in the baked loaf of white bread to no more than 38%. It also restricts the use of nonwheat flours to "not more than 3 parts for each 100 parts by weight of flour used." Other paragraphs of this regulation control the addition of dough conditioners and other additives, including enrichment. This part of the regulation also defines "bread" as weighing "one-half pound or more after cooling." Smaller units are defined as "rolls" or "buns."

The basic formulation for white pan bread is relatively simple. Because retail bakers tend to use a more basic formulation with fewer additives, they generally prefer a slightly "stronger" flour (12-13% protein) than the large bread bakeries. Major producers of white pan bread usually utilize dough strengthening ingredients in conjunction with flour containing about 11.5% protein.

Nonfat milk solids and milk replacers are used more to improve the toasting quality of bread rather than to upgrade its nutritional value. The 4% (f.b.) lard used in bread products before the 1970s has long since been replaced with 2% (f.b.) of the more "consumer friendly" vegetable oil. To speed up the mixing process, the addition of salt is often delayed until the gluten is partially developed. This, however, requires a very soluble salt.

Although the basic formulation of white pan bread is not affected by the dough-making technology, the use of dough oxidants and dough conditioners can vary significantly with manufacturing conditions.

As the name implies, "white pan bread" is baked in rectangular pans, which used to be manufactured from tin-plated steel. This has led many retail bakers to refer to *baking tins* when they talk about baking pans. To reduce the reflection of radiated heat from the shiny coating of "tinned" pans, these pans used to be "burnt in" according to a complex and lengthy procedure. This treatment of new pans has, however, been replaced by special darker coatings applied to new baking pans at the time of their manufacture. One fact worth remembering: the tin plating melts at a temperature of 449°F (232°C). Therefore, empty tin-plated bread pans should never be placed in, or conveyed through, a hot oven! If there are only three loaves in a 4-pan strap, the empty pan must be filled with scrap dough or with some other heat absorbing material before the strap of pans is loaded into the oven.

During the 1950s pan manufacturers introduced *aluminized steel* pans. These pans can tolerate temperatures up to 1,000°F (534°C) and they will resist corrosion (rusting). Aluminized steel is made from the same type of steel as tin-plated pans. But, instead of being tin-plated, the steel is laminated to a thin layer of an aluminum alloy. The aluminized steel pans can be, and generally are, coated to provide a darker surface for improved heat absorption. These pans can be glazed and have the same release properties as tin-plated pans. The performance of aluminized steel pans in bakery production has been so satisfying that they have become the "standard" in the baking industry. Most pan manufacturers no longer manufacture tin-plated pans.

Formula 1
White Pan Bread
(No-Time Straight Dough)

Baker's Percent	Weight lb.	oz.	Ingredients
100	6	4	Bread Flour (12% Protein)
6		6	Granulated Sugar
4		4	Nonfat Dry Milk
2		2	Salt
0.5		0.5	Mineral Yeast Food
0.006	(60 ppm)		Ascorbic Acid
3		3	Bread Shortening
3.5		3.5	Compressed Yeast
64	4	0	Water (Variable)
183.006	**11**	**7.006**	**Total Amount**

Mix:	To full gluten development.
Dough Temperature:	82°F (28°C).
Floor Time:	10 minutes.
Scaling Weight:	18.5 oz (525 g) per 1 lb. (454 g) loaf.
Proof:	About 60 minutes at 109°F (43°C) to full proof.
Bake:	16 to 18 minutes at 450°F (232°C).
Cool:	One hour under ambient conditions on cooling rack.

Formula 2
White Pan Bread
(Fermented Straight Dough)

Baker's Percent	Weight lb.	oz.	Ingredients
100	6	4	Bread Flour (12% Protein)
6		6	Granulated Sugar
2		2	Nonfat Dry Milk
2		2	Salt
0.5		0.5	Mineral Yeast Food
3		3	Bread Shortening
3		3	Compressed Yeast
62	3	14	Water (Variable)
178.5	**11**	**2.5**	**Total Amount**

Mix: To full gluten development.

Dough Temperature: 78-80°F (25.5-26.5°C).

Fermentation (Floor) Time: 1-1.5 hours at 84°F (29°C).

Scaling Weight: 18.5 oz (525 g) per 1 lb. (454 g) loaf.

Proof: About 60 minutes at 109°F (43°C) to full proof.

Bake: 16-18 minutes at 450°F (232°C).

Cool: One hour under ambient conditions on cooling rack.

Formula 3
White Pan Bread
(Sponge and Dough Method)

Baker's Percent	Weight lb.	oz.	Ingredients
	Sponge: (Preferment)		
70	4	6	Bread Flour (11.5% Protein)
0.5		0.5	Mineral Yeast Food
0.5		0.5	Sodium Stearoyl Lactylate
2.5		2.5	Compressed Yeast
42	2	10	Water
	Dough: (Remix)		
30	1	14	Bread Flour (11.5% Protein)
9		9	42% High-Fructose Corn Syrup (71% solids)
2		2	Milk Replacer
2		2	Salt
3		3	Bread Shortening
1		1	Crumb Softener (Hydrated)
15		15	Water and Ice (Variable)
177.5	**11**	**1.5**	**Total Amount**

Sponge: *Temperature:* 74-77°F (24-25°C).
Fermentation Time: 3.5-4 hours at 84°F (29°C).

Dough: *Mix:* To full gluten development.
Temperature: 78-80°F (25.5-26.5°C).
Floor Time: 10-15 minutes under ambient conditions.

Scaling Weight: 112-117% of desired baked weight.

Proof: About 60 minutes at 109°F (43°C) to full proof.

Bake: 1 lb. loaves: 16 to 18 minutes at 450°F (232°C)
1 1/4 and 1 1/2 lb. loaves: 18 to 24 minutes at 450°F.

Cool: One hour under ambient conditions on rack or conveyor.

Formula 4
White Pan Bread
(40% Flour Liquid Sponge and Dough Method)

Baker's Percent	Weight lb.	oz.	Ingredients
Liquid Sponge: (Preferment)			
40	2	8	Bread Flour (11.5% Protein)
0.5		0.5	Salt
0.5		0.5	Sodium Stearoyl Lactylate
0.25		0.25	Monocalcium Phosphate
0.063		0.06	Ammonium Sulfate
0.009	(90 ppm)		Ascorbic Acid
3		3	Compressed Yeast
50.3	3	2.3	Water
Dough: (Remix)			
60	3	12	Bread Flour (11.5% Protein)
8.5		8.5	42% High-Fructose Corn Syrup (71% Solids)
2		2	Milk Replacer
1.5		1.5	Salt
2		2	Vegetable Oil
1		1	Crumb Softener (Hydrated)
7.5		7.5	Water and Ice (Variable)
177.122	11	1.11	Total Amount

Liquid Sponge: *Initial Temperature:* 80°F (27°C).
Fermentation Time: 2 hours at 84°F (29°C).
Holding Temperature: 41°F (5°C).

Dough: *Mix:* To full gluten development.
Temperature: 78-80°F (25.5-26.5°C).
Fermentation (Floor) Time: 15 minutes.

Scaling Weight: 112 to 117% of desired baked weight.

Proof: About 55 minutes at 109°F (43°C) to full proof.

Bake: 1 lb. loaves: 16 to 18 minutes at 450°F (232°C).
1 1/4 and 1 1/2 lb. loaves: 18 to 24 minutes at 450°F.

Cool: One hour under ambient conditions on cooling rack.

Formula 5
White Pan Bread
(No Flour Water Brew and Dough Method)

Baker's Percent	Weight lb.	oz.	Ingredients
	Water Brew Ferment		
3		3	42% High-Fructose Corn Syrup (71% Solids)
0.5		0.5	Salt
0.2		0.2	Fermentation Buffer*
3		3	Compressed Yeast
43.5	2	11.5	Water
	Dough		
100	6	4	Bread Flour (11.5% Protein)
10		10	42% High-Fructose Corn Syrup (71% Solids)
2		2	Milk Replacer
1.5		1.5	Salt
0.06		0.06	Ammonium Sulfate
0.25		0.25	Monocalcium Phosphate
0.5		0.5	Sodium Stearoyl Lactylate
3		3	Bread Shortening
0.009	(90 ppm)		Ascorbic Acid
16.8	1	0.8	Water and Ice (Variable)
184.319	**11**	**8.31**	**Total Amount**

*Fermentation Buffer: Ingredient Legend: Calcium carbonate, ammonium sulfate, flour, salt and calcium sulfate.

Water Brew: *Initial Temperature:* 80°F (27°C)
Ferment: *Fermentation Time:* 2 hours at 84°F (29°C).
Holding Temperature: 41°F (5°C).
Dough: *Mix:* To full gluten development.
Temperature: 78-80°F (25.5-26.5°C).
Floor Time: 15 minutes at ambient temperature.
Scaling Weight: 112-117% of desired baked weight.
Proof: About 55 minutes at 109°F (43°C) to full proof.
Bake: 1 lb. (454 gram) loaves: 16-18 minutes at 450°F.
1 1/4 and 1 1/2 loaves: 18-24 minutes at 450°F.
Cool: One hour under ambient conditions on rack or conveyor.

Wheat Breads

Wheat Bread contains a variable amount of whole wheat flour and the remainder is white flour. However, the Standard of Identity (21 CFR Chapter I, Part 136.180) mandates that *Whole Wheat Bread* be prepared from only whole wheat flour and without any white flour. But the standard of identity does not rule out the use of some vital wheat gluten in whole wheat bread.

Whole wheat flour contains the wheat germ with a fat content of 10-11%. Since most of the fat in the germ is polyunsaturated, the shelf-life of whole wheat flour depends on the storage conditions for this flour. Warmer temperatures and high humidity promote rancidity in this type of flour. Whole wheat will also develop a bitter taste with time. This bitter taste can be easily noticed in whole wheat bread and in any product prepared with a significant amount of whole wheat flour or bran. The bitterness tends to be stronger in finely ground whole wheat flour than in the coarser meals.

Even under ideal cool and dry storage conditions, whole wheat flour should not be stored for more than three months. This time is reduced to only one month if the flour is finely ground and stored in a warm bakeshop. The baker must not only avoid overstocking, but must also watch that the supply of whole wheat flour is properly rotated, i.e., the oldest flour must be used first. Also, as a general rule, the finer the particle size of the whole wheat, the more rapidly the eating quality of the flour tends to deteriorate.

The coarse ground whole wheat needs more time to hydrate than the finely ground flour. The coarse whole wheat flour will also give the bread a more "grainy" mouthfeel and a lower loaf volume. For these reasons this flour is well suited for the denser and more "rustic" (as made on farms from home-ground wheat) breads. Because the coarser meals retain their identity better in the finished product, they are also used by many bakers in their regular wheat bread. Overall, the medium and coarse whole wheat flours produce, for most consumers, a more pleasant taste and mouthfeel in wheat and whole wheat breads.

The finely ground whole wheat flour performs more like regular white flour than the coarser meals. Its particle size is small enough for most of the protein in the flour fraction to develop into gluten. This is not the case with coarse ground particles in which much of the protein is physically bound to fragments of the original grain. The finely ground whole wheat flour, milled or stone ground, will, therefore, produce larger loaf volumes with the same amount of vital wheat gluten added to the dough. Whereas medium and coarse whole wheat flour require about 5% wheat gluten for sufficient loaf volume, fine whole wheat flour will produce the same loaf volume with only 3% wheat gluten and with 3 to 4% (f.b.) extra water.

Cracked, cut, and rolled wheat are not suitable for whole wheat bread, but these whole wheat products perform well in wheat breads. Because of their granulation size, these wheat derivatives require a long hydration time and will retain some of their identity in the finished product. If these whole wheat ingredients cannot be properly hydrated in a preferment, they must be soaked for 30-60 minutes in room temperature water before they can be added to the mix. This is especially important when these wheat breads are produced by the no-time dough method.

Formula 6
Whole Wheat Bread
(Sponge and Dough Method)

Baker's Percent	Weight lb.	oz.	Ingredients
			Sponge: (Preferment)
65	4	1	Whole Wheat Flour (Medium)
5		5	Vital Wheat Gluten
0.5		0.5	Mineral Yeast Food
0.5		0.5	Sodium Stearoyl Lactylate
2.5		2.5	Compressed Yeast
0.009	(90 ppm)		Ascorbic Acid
43	2	11	Water
			Dough: (Remix)
30	1	14	Whole Wheat Flour (Medium)
8		8	Brown Sugar
2		2	Milk Replacer
2		2	Salt
3		3	Bread Shortening
20	1	4	Water and Ice (Variable)
181.509	**11**	**5.5**	**Total Amount**

Sponge: *Temperature:* 74-77°F (24-25°C).
Fermentation Time: 3.5 to 4 hours at 84°F (29°C).

Dough: *Mix:* To full gluten development (Please note: whole wheat flour doughs tend to develop more quickly than white bread doughs and they also have less mixing tolerance).
Temperature: 78-80°F (25.5-26.5°C).
Floor Time: 10 to 15 min. under ambient conditions.

Scaling Weight: 115-117% of desired baked weight. (Please note: for best results use slightly smaller pans for whole wheat bread than for white pan bread).

Proof: About 60 minutes at 109°F (43°C) to full proof.

Bake: 1 lb. loaves: 18-20 minutes at 430°F (221°C).
1 1/4 and 1 1/2 lb. loaves: 21-28 minutes at 430°F.

Cool: One hour under ambient conditions on rack or conveyor.

Formula 6A
Whole Wheat Bread
(No-Time Dough Method)

Baker's Percent	Weight lb.	oz.	Ingredients
95	5	15	Whole Wheat Flour (Medium)
5		5	Vital Wheat Gluten
8		8	Brown Sugar
2		2	Nonfat Dry Milk
2		2	Salt
0.5		0.5	Sodium Stearoyl Lactylate
0.5		0.5	Mineral Yeast Food
3		3	Bread Shortening
3.5		3.5	Compressed Yeast
0.009	(90 ppm)		Ascorbic Acid
66	4	2	Water and Ice
185.509	**11**	**9.5**	**Total Amount**

Mix: To full gluten development.
Dough Temperature: 82°F (28°C).
Floor Time: 10 minutes.
Dough Scaling Weight: 18.5 ounces (525 grams) per 1 pound (454 gram) loaf.
Proof: About 60 minutes at 110°F (43°C) to full proof.
Bake: 1 pound loaves: 18-20 minutes at 430°F (221°C).
Cool: One hour under ambient conditions on rack or conveyor.

Formula 7
Honey Wheat Bread

Baker's Percent	Weight lb.	oz.	Ingredients
		Sponge: (Preferment)	
30	1	14	Rolled Wheat Flour*
40	2	8	Bread Flour
0.5		0.5	Sodium Stearoyl Lactylate
0.5		0.5	Mineral Yeast Food
2.5		2.5	Compressed Yeast
0.006		(60 ppm)	Ascorbic Acid
42	2	10	Water
		Dough: (Remix)	
30	1	14	Bread Flour
2		2	Salt
10		10	Liquid Honey
3		3	Bread Shortening
15.3		15.3	Water and Ice
175.806	10	15.8	Total Amount

*Medium or coarse whole wheat flour may be substituted for the rolled wheat flour.

Sponge: *Temperature:* 74-77°F (24 to 25°C).
Fermentation Time: 3.5 to 4 hours at 84°F (29°C)
Dough: *Mix:* To full gluten development.
Temperature: 78-80°F (25.5-26.5°C).
Floor Time: 10-15 minutes under ambient conditions.
**Scaling
Weight:** 115-117% of desired baked weight.
Proof: About 60 minutes at 109°F (43°C) to full proof.
Bake: 1 lb. loaves: 16 to 18 minutes at 450°F (232°C).
1 1/4 and 1 1/2 lb. loaves: 20-28 minutes at 430°F.

Note: *Honey Wheat Bread* may also be produced by the no-time bread making method by combining all ingredients, increasing the compressed yeast to 3.5% (f.b.), and by increasing the ascorbic acid to 90 ppm (f.b.). A slight upward adjustment in the dough water amount may also be necessary. The dough temperature should be 80 to 82°F (27 to 28°C).

The honey in this formulation may be replaced with brown sugar or a combination of brown sugar and light molasses. When this is done, however, the word "honey" must be deleted from the name of this bread.

Formula 8
Cracked Wheat Bread
(No-Time Dough Method)

Baker's Percent	Weight lb.	oz.	Ingredients
			Soaked Grain: (one hour)
35	2	3	Cracked (Cut) Wheat
35	2	3	Water (75°F or 24°C)
			Dough: (Mix)
65	4	1	Bread Flour
4		4	Brown Sugar
5		5	Light Molasses
2		2	Salt
0.5		0.5	Sodium Stearoyl Lactylate
0.5		0.5	Mineral Yeast Food
3		3	Bread Shortening
3.5		3.5	Compressed Yeast
0.009	(90 ppm)		Ascorbic Acid
23	1	7	Water and Ice
176.509	**11**	**0.5**	**Total Amount**

Mix:	To full gluten development.
Dough Temperature:	80-82°F (27-28°C).
Floor Time:	10 minutes.
Scaling Weight:	18.5 ounces (525 grams) dough per 1 lb. (454 grams) bread.
Proof:	60-65 minutes at 109°F (43°C) to full proof.
Bake:	16-18 min. at 450°F (232°C).
Cool:	One hour under ambient conditions on rack or conveyor.

Formula 9
Honey Bran Bread
(Sponge and Dough Method)

Baker's Percent	Weight lb.	oz.	Ingredients
			Sponge: (Preferment)
42	2	10	Bread Flour
25	1	9	Wheat Bran
3		3	Vital Wheat Gluten
0.5		0.5	Sodium Stearoyl Lactylate
0.5		0.5	Mineral Yeast Food
2.5		2.5	Compressed Yeast
0.006	(60 ppm)		Ascorbic Acid
50	3	2	Water
			Dough: (Remix)
30	1	14	Bread Flour
10		10	Liquid Honey
2		2	Nonfat Dry Milk
2		2	Salt
3		3	Bread Shortening
16	1	0	Water and Ice
186.506	**11**	**10.5**	**Total Amount**

Sponge: *Temperature:* 74-77°F (24 to 25°C).
Fermentation Time: 3.5-4 hours at 84°F (29°C).

Dough: *Mix:* to full gluten development.
Temperature: 78-80°F (25.5-26.5°C).
Floor Time: 10-15 minutes under ambient conditions.

Scaling Weight: 18.5 ounces (525 grams) dough per 1 lb. (454 gram) bread.

Proof: 60-65 minutes at 109°F (43°C) to full proof.

Bake: 1 lb. Loaves: 16-18 minutes at 450°F (232°C).

Cool: One hour under ambient conditions on rack or conveyor.

Multigrain Bread

Multigrain implies that the bread is made from components of several grains in addition to wheat. Non-wheat grain proteins do not form gluten during mixing. In order to give their multigrain doughs more strength, bakers generally add vital wheat gluten to doughs in which more than 10% of the wheat flour has been replaced with non-wheat grains. A good starting point for the level of wheat gluten used is one part vital wheat gluten for every five parts of non-wheat grain. The baker may, however, choose to add more or less wheat gluten, depending on the types of grain used and how much loaf volume is desired.

Although barley, buckwheat, corn, flaxseed, millet, oat, poppy, rice, rye, sesame, and triticale are widely recognized as grains, there are some reservations about counting de-fatted soybean flour as one of the multi-grain components.

Whereas finely ground particles of many grains tend to lose their physical identity in the finished product, larger particles, like hulled millet and sunflower seed kernels, are readily identifiable and tend to produce small holes in the crumb structure.

Flaxseed should be used in the milled form for maximum nutritional benefit (Anonymous 1994). Without milling, the alpha linolenic (omega-3) polyunsaturated fatty acids and the lignans (a beneficial steroid-like substance) in the seed are not readily absorbed by the human digestive system. However, because the polyunsaturated fatty acids in the milled seeds are exposed to oxygen in the air, milled flaxseed has a very short shelf-life and must be stored either under vacuum or in an inert atmosphere to prevent rancidity and off-flavor development. Because of its dark color, flaxseed is best used in dark breads. While whole flaxseed has little, if any, effect on loaf volume, milled flaxseed has a depressing effect on loaf volume and should be used with caution.

Other grain products having an adverse effect on loaf volume are wheat bran, corn flour, and barley derivatives (e.g. pearled barley and barley flakes). However, the effect of these products is relatively mild in comparison to the effect of milled flaxseed and soy flour.

When grains have a color different from wheat, the particle size will determine whether the grains are noticed either as specks or as an off-color in the crumb. While yellow corn flour will tint the crumb yellow, rye will give the bread a gray cast. Barley and oat ingredients will darken the crumb color only very slightly. The same holds true for the light buckwheat flour, while the dark buckwheat flour used at the 10% flour replacement level causes a significant darkening of the crumb color. In order to mask all these off-colors, bakers often add molasses as a sweetener, which gives the crumb a nice medium brown color. A light molasses flavor also tends to complement the taste of the various grains.

Like whole wheat breads, multi-grain breads are generally more dense than regular white pan bread and thus should be baked in pans 10-15% smaller than used for white bread and for a slightly longer time at a lower temperature (430°F or 221°C). Bakers lacking smaller pan sizes may increase the weight of their dark breads to the next legal size, e.g. from 16 to 20 ounces finished weight.

Most bakers prefer to use commercially available multi-grain mixes. There are many excellent mixes on the market. The manufacturers of these mixes will often also supply the baker with beautifully designed packaging and display materials, provided the baker uses the mixes or concentrates as suggested. The baker may even prefer to prepare a unique blend of grains. However, there is no magic combination of grains which spells success.

The following three multi-grain blends are significantly different from each other and may serve as suggested starter formulations for bakers who do not mind experimenting and keeping special ingredients in inventory. These multigrain blends are usually used to replace 20 to 30% of the flour. At these levels, however, it is also advisable to add 3 to 5% of vital wheat gluten to the mix. Without the extra wheat gluten, the loaves of bread will be of very low volume.

Multi-Grain Blends

Ingredient:	Blend A 10 Grain %	Blend B 7 Grain %	Blend C 7 Grain %
Rolled Wheat	-	-	60
Quick Wheat Flakes	17	20	-
Rolled Oat Flakes	17	20	10
Rolled Rye Flakes	13	16	10
Milled Flaxseed	10	12	6
Dark Buckwheat Flour	7	-	4
Light Buckwheat Flour	-	8	-
Barley Grits	10	12	-
Coarse Corn Flour	10	12	6
Sunflower Kernels	7	-	4
Hulled Millet	3	-	-
Roasted Sesame Seed	6	-	-
Total Percent	100	100	100
Usage Level (f.b.)	30	25	50
Use with Wheat Gluten	5	5	5

Formula 10
Multi-Grain Bread
(Sponge and Dough Method)

Baker's Percent	Weight lb.	oz.	Ingredients
			Sponge: (Preferment)
25	1	9	Multi-Grain Blend
40	2	8	Bread Flour
5		5	Vital Wheat Gluten
0.5		0.5	Mineral Yeast Food
2.5		2.5	Compressed Yeast
0.006	(60 ppm)		Ascorbic Acid
42	2	10	Water
			Dough: (Remix)
30	1	14	Bread Flour
10		10	Liquid Honey
2		2	Dry Milk Solids or Replacer
2		2	Salt
3		3	Bread Shortening
14.2		14.2	Water and Ice
176.206	**11**	**0.2**	**Total Amount**

Sponge: *Temperature:* 74-77°F (24-25°C).
Fermentation Time: 3.5-4 hours at 84°F (29°C).
Dough: *Mix:* To full gluten development.
Temperature: 78-80°F (25.5-26.5°C).
Floor Time: 10-15 minutes under ambient conditions.
Scaling Weight: 18.5 ounces (525 grams) dough per 1 pound (454 gram) loaf.
Proof: About 60 minutes at 109°F (43°C) to full proof.
Bake: 1 lb. Loaves: 16 to 18 minutes at 450°F (232°C).
Cool: One hour under ambient conditions on rack or conveyor.

Please note: The multi-grain blend may be from a commercial source or be the baker's own proprietary blend. Its proportion in the total flour mix may be increased or decreased slightly without any major adjustment in the formulation, other than minor changes in dough water absorption.

Raisin Bread

The Code of Federal Regulations (21 CFR Ch. I) specifies under paragraph 136.160 that: (1) Not less than 50 parts by weight of seeded or seedless raisins are used for each 100 parts by weight of flour used; and that (2) Water extract of raisins may be used, but not to replace raisins.

For best results, the raisins must be properly "conditioned" prior to their addition to the dough. There are many different procedures used by bakers, some of which are quite wasteful. Raisins should never be soaked in an excessive amount of water, so that some of the water must be discarded. During soaking much of the sugar and flavor in the raisins is leached by the water and lost when this water is discarded.

The best method for soaking raisins is to place them in a narrow upright container and to add one part of room temperature water for every four parts of raisins. After compressing the raisins slightly in the container, almost all of them are immersed in free water. Most of this water will be absorbed within one hour of soaking time. The raisins will be plump, but never too soft for incorporation into a bread dough.

Formula 11
Raisin Bread
(Sponge and Dough Method)

Baker's Percent	Weight lb.	oz.	Ingredients
			Sponge: (Preferment)
67	4	3	Bread Flour
3		3	Vital Wheat Gluten
0.5		0.5	Mineral Yeast Food
2.5		2.5	Compressed Yeast
44	2	12	Water
			Dough: (Remix)
30	1	14	Bread Flour
6		6	Granulated or Brown Sugar
2		2	Nonfat Dry Milk or Replacer
2		2	Salt
0.1		0.1	Cinnamon
3		3	Bread Shortening
1		1	Compressed Yeast
10		10	Water and Ice
			Soaked Raisins: (1 Hour Soak)
50	3	2	Raisins
12.5		12.5	Water (77°F or 25°C)
233.6	**14**	**9.6**	**Total Amount**

Sponge: *Temperature:* 74 to 77°F (24 to 25°C).
Fermentation Time: 3.5 to 4 hours at 84°F (29°C).

Dough: *Mix* dough without raisins to full gluten development.
Add soaked raisins with all liquids not absorbed by the raisins.
Mix: 0.5 minute at low speed and about one minute at medium speed to incorporate the raisins into the dough. **Do not mix the dough with the raisins more than absolutely necessary!**
Temperature: 78 to 80°F (25.5 to 26.5°C).
Floor Time: 10 to 15 minutes under ambient conditions.

Scaling Weight: 115-117% of desired baked weight. Note: Raisin bread should be baked in smaller pans than used for white pan bread.

Proof: 60-70 minutes at 109°F (43°C) to full proof.

Bake: 1 1/4 pound (568 gram) loaves: 21-24 minutes at 410°F (210°C).

Cool: One hour under ambient conditions on rack or conveyor.

Formula 12
Raisin Bran Bread
(Sponge and Dough Method)

Baker's Percent	Weight lb.	oz	Ingredients
			Sponge: (Preferment)
50	3	2	Bread Flour
15		15	Wheat Bran
5		5	Vital Wheat Gluten
0.5		0.5	Mineral Yeast Food
3		3	Compressed Yeast
0.006	(60 ppm)		Ascorbic Acid
47	2	15	Water
			Dough: (Remix)
30	1	14	Bread Flour
6		6	Granulated or Brown Sugar
2		2	Nonfat Dry Milk
2		2	Salt
3		3	Bread Shortening
1		1	Compressed Yeast
8		8	Water and Ice
			Soaked Raisins: (1 Hour Soak)
50	3	2	Raisins
12.5		12.5	Water
235.006	**14**	**11**	**Total Amount**

Sponge: *Temperature:* 74-77°F (24-25°C).
Fermentation Time: 3.5-4 hours at 84°F (29°C)

Dough: *Mix* dough without raisins to full gluten development.
Add soaked raisins with all liquids not absorbed by the raisins.
Mix 0.5 minutes at low speed and about one minute at medium speed to incorporate the raisins into the dough. **Do not mix the dough with the raisins more than absolutely necessary!**
Temperature: 78-80°F (25.5-26.5°C).
Floor Time: 10-15 minutes under ambient conditions.

Scaling Weight: 115 to 117% of desired baked weight.

Proof: 60-70 minutes at 109°F ((43°C) to full proof.

Bake: 1¼ lb. (568 gram) loaves: 21-24 minutes at 410°F (210°C).

Cool: One hour under ambient conditions on rack or conveyor.

Oatmeal Bread

Oatmeal added to bread dough at the 20% flour replacement level gives bread a unique flavor. A small amount of cinnamon added to the dough will help to accentuate this flavor. Replacing an additional 20% of the bread flour with coarse or medium grind whole wheat will not only improve the flavor of the bread, but also the texture of the crumb. Although the suggested formula specifies *rolled oats*, oat flakes may also be used. Like any coarse grain product, the rolled oats are best added to the preferment for better hydration. Rolled oats will slightly reduce the dough water absorption.

Formula 13
Oatmeal Bread
(Sponge and Dough Method)

Baker's Percent	Weight lb.	oz.	Ingredients
			Sponge: (Preferment)
45	2	13	Bread Flour
20	1	4	Rolled Oats
5		5	Vital Wheat Gluten
0.5		0.5	Sodium Stearoyl Lactylate
0.5		0.5	Mineral Yeast Food
2.5		2.5	Compressed Yeast
0.009		(90 ppm)	Ascorbic Acid
40	2	8	Water
			Dough: (Remix)
10		10	Bread Flour
20	1	4	Whole Wheat Flour (Coarse)
4		4	Granulated or Brown Sugar
10		10	Liquid Honey
2		2	Nonfat Dry Milk
2		2	Salt
0.05		0.05	Cinnamon
3		3	Bread Shortening
1		1	Compressed Yeast
16	1	0	Water and Ice
181.559	11	5.55	**Total Amount**

Sponge: *Temperature:* 74-77°F (24-25°C).
Fermentation Time: 3.5-4 hours at 84°F (29°C).

Dough: *Mix:* To full gluten development.
Temperature: 78-80°F (25.5-26.5°C).
Floor Time: 10-15 minuntes under ambient conditions.

Scaling Weight: 18.5 ounces (525 grams) dough per 1 pound (454 gram) loaf.

Proof: About 60 minutes at 109°F (43°C) to full proof.

Bake: 1 lb. loaves: 16-18 minutes at 450°F (232°C).

Wheat 'n' Rye Bread

The combination of pumpernickel rye and whole wheat flour makes this bread different from regular pan breads and ideal for sandwiches. Although finely ground flours tend to give more loaf volume, the coarser meals provide a more satisfying taste and a better mouthfeel.

Formula 14
Wheat 'n' Rye Bread
(Sponge and Dough Method)

Baker's Percent	Weight lb.	oz.	Ingredients
			Sponge: (Preferment)
45	2	13	Whole Wheat Flour (Medium)
20	1	4	Pumpernickel Rye Meal (Coarse)
5		5	Vital Wheat Gluten
0.5		0.5	Sodium Stearoyl Lactylate
0.5		0.5	Mineral Yeast Food
3		3	Compressed Yeast
0.006	(60 ppm)		Ascorbic Acid
42	2	10	Water
			Dough: (Remix)
30	1	14	Bread Flour
8		8	Brown Sugar
2		2	Nonfat Dry Milk or Replacer
2		2	Salt
3		3	Bread Shortening
16	1	0	Water and Ice
177.006	**11**	**1**	**Total Amount**

Sponge: *Temperature:* 74-77°F (24-25°C).
Fermentation Time: 3.5-4 hours at 84°F (29°C).

Dough: *Mix:* To full gluten development.
Temperature: 78 to 80°F (25.5 to 26.5°C).
Floor Time: 10 to 15 minutes under ambient conditions.

Scaling Weight: 18.5 ounces (525 grams) dough per 1 pound (454 gram) loaf.

Proof: 60-70 minutes at 109°F (43°C) to full proof.

Bake: 1 lb. Loaves: 16-18 minutes at 450°F (232°C).

Cool: One hour under ambient conditions on rack or conveyor.

Rustic Breads

Rustic breads have become very popular in central Europe and are perceived as "healthy." This type of bread is dense, made from whole wheat and other grains, and is baked for a longer time at low heat. Because of their dough characteristics and low loaf volumes, rustic breads are usually prepared as round loaves. The thick crust keeps the loaves fresh longer, even when left unprotected. However, for easier slicing, it is recommended that the loaves be stored in plastic bags or in a closed container which keeps the crust slightly softer.

Formula 15
Farmer's Bread
(Sponge and Dough Method)

Baker's Percent	Weight lb.	oz.	Ingredients
			Sponge: (Preferment)
50	3	2	Rolled Wheat
20	1	4	Pumpernickel Rye Meal (Coarse)
0.5		0.5	Mineral Yeast Food
2.5		2.5	Compressed Yeast
42	2	10	Water
			Dough: (Remix)
20	1	4	Whole Wheat Flour (Medium)
5		5	Corn Flour (coarse)
5		5	Light Buckwheat Flour
4		4	Brown Sugar
2		2	Salt
2		2	Bread Shortening
16	1	0	Water and Ice
169	**10**	**9**	**Total Amount**

Sponge: *Temperature:* 74-77°F (24-25°C).
Fermentation Time: 3.5 to 4 hours at 84°F (29°C).

Dough: *Mix:* Until dough is developed.
Temperature: 78-80°F (25.5-26.5°C).
Floor Time: 10 minutes under ambient conditions

Scaling Weight: 36 ounces (1020 grams) dough per 2 lb. (908 gram) loaf. Mould into a round loaf.

Proof: About 60 minutes at 109°F (43°C).
Note: After 40 to 45 minutes of proof time, make two parallel cuts with a sharp knife or blade across the surface of round loaves and cross these cuts with two more parallel cuts. These cuts are primarily for a decorative purpose and may not be deeper than 1/4 inch (6 to 7 millimeter).

Bake: 55 to 60 minutes at 400°F (205°C).

Formula 16
Swiss Peasant Bread
(Sponge and Dough Method)

Baker's Percent	Weight lb.	oz.	Ingredients
			Sponge: (Preferment)
52.5	3	4.5	Whole Wheat Flour (Medium)
7.5		7.5	Rolled Oat Flakes
10		10	Pumpernickel Rye Meal (Coarse)
0.5		0.5	Mineral Yeast Food
2.5		2.5	Compressed Yeast
42	2	10	Water
			Dough: (Remix)
15		15	Whole Wheat Flour (Medium)
5		5	Corn Flour (Coarse)
5		5	Light Buckwheat Flour
3		3	Milled Flaxseed
2		2	Sunflower Kernels
4		4	Brown Sugar
2		2	Nonfat Dry Milk
2.1		2.1	Salt
2		2	Bread Shortening
15		15	Water and Ice
170.1	**10**	**10.1**	**Total Amount**

Sponge: *Temperature:* 74-77°F (24-25°C).
Fermentation Time: 3.5-4 hours at 84°F (29°C).

Dough: *Mix:* Until dough is developed. Do not overmix!
Temperature: 78-80°F (25.5-26.5°C).
Floor Time: 10 minutes under ambient conditions.

Scaling Weight: 36 ounces (1020 grams) dough per 2 pound (908 gram) loaf. Mould into a round loaf.

Proof: About 60 minutes at 109°F (43°C).
Note: After 40 to 45 minutes proof time, make two parallel cuts with a sharp knife or blade across the surface of the round loaves and cross these cuts with two more parallel cuts. These cuts are primarily for a decorative purpose and may not be deeper than 1/4 inch (6 to 7 millimeter).

Bake: 50 to 55 minutes at 400°F (205°C).

High-Fiber Bread

There are a large number of high-fiber ingredients available to bakers. The varieties range from bran and cell wall material to cellulose fiber manufactured from wood or cottonseed lint. Unless the dietary fiber in bran is further concentrated by refining, its fiber content is usually not high enough to produce *reduced calorie* bakery foods. To make this claim, the "reduced calorie bread" must contain at least 25% less calories than an equivalent full-calorie reference product. For a significant calorie reduction, it is recommended to use ingredients with a dietary fiber content of at least 85%, excluding soluble fiber.

In choosing the fiber ingredient, the baker must be aware of the fact that some of the vegetable fiber ingredients may not only contribute to the finished product color and taste, but that these ingredients may also adversely affect other bread quality characteristics. Unless marketing requires the use of fiber ingredients made from corn bran or cell wall material from soybeans or peas, cellulose fiber will usually produce the best results in calorie reduced breads.

The non-wheat components and the increased dough water content in reduced calorie bread will generally result in reduced bread volume. To overcome this shortcoming, bakers add vital wheat gluten and a small amount of a film-forming gum to doughs in which a significant amount of wheat flour has been replaced with non-wheat ingredients. The film-forming gums (carboxymethyl cellulose, guar gum, etc.) are usually used at the level of 0.3-1.0% (f.b.). The vital wheat gluten is added at levels of one part gluten for every 2.5 to 3 parts of dietary fiber ingredient. The functionality of the wheat gluten can, however, be significantly enhanced by the addition of a small amount (approximately 0.5% f.b.) of diacetyl tartaric acid esters of monoglycerides, thus requiring the addition of up to 30% less wheat gluten.

Most high-fiber ingredients can be added either to the sponge (preferment) or at the dough (remix) stage. However, some coarse fiber products benefit from the longer hydration time in the preferment.

Doughs prepared with high-fiber ingredients must be mixed to full gluten development, which is not always easy to determine without a series of test bakes. Undermixed and overmixed doughs will produce bread with a lower loaf volume.

Because of the higher moisture content in doughs prepared with high-fiber ingredients, bread baked from these doughs should be baked slightly longer and at a lower temperature than white pan bread.

Formula 17
High Fiber Pan Bread

Baker's Percent	Weight lb.	oz.	Ingredients
			Sponge: (Preferment)
54.3	3	6.3	Bread Flour
6.2		6.2	Vital Wheat Gluten
0.5		0.5	Mineral Yeast Food
2.8		2.8	Compressed Yeast
40	2	8	Water
			Dough: (Remix)
23.2	1	7.2	Bread Flour
16.3	1	0.3	High-Fiber Ingredient
5.5		5.5	Granulated Sugar
2		2	Salt
0.2		0.2	Carboxymethyl Cellulose Gum
0.5		0.5	Crumb Softener (Monoglyceride)
0.009		(90 ppm)	Ascorbic Acid
54	3	6	Water and Ice
205.509	**12**	**13.5**	**Total Amount**

Sponge: *Temperature:* 74-77°F (24-25°C).
Fermentation Time: 3.5-4 hours at 84°F (29°C).

Dough: *Mix:* To full gluten development.
Temperature: 78-80°F (25.5-26.5°C).
Floor Time: 10-15 minutes under ambient conditions.

Scaling Weight: 18.5 ounces (525 grams) dough per 1 pound (454 gram) loaf.

Proof: About 60 minutes at 109°F (43°C) to full proof.

Bake: 1 lb. loaves: 18 minutes at 435°F (224°C).

Cool: One hour under ambient conditions on rack or conveyor.

Hearth-Baked White Breads

Although there is a wide variety of breads on the market which are baked directly on the oven hearth or in perforated metal trays or pans, French, Italian, and Vienna breads are the main representatives of this bread category. True French and Italian breads are made from only the basic four bread ingredients: flour, water, yeast, and salt. The Vienna bread usually contains some shortening, milk and eggs. Some bakers even add a small amount of potato flour to their Vienna bread doughs. The potato flour tends to soften and tenderize the bread crumb. But in the overall effort to extend the shelf-life and eating quality of the bread, most bakers now add a very small amount of shortening and sugar even to the French and Italian breads, so that the only real difference between these three types of hearth-baked bread is primarily their make-up and appearance.

The French bread is generally shaped into long and narrow loaves (baguettes) which often are broken or cut diagonally into pieces rather than sliced. Its shelf-life is very short and limited to a few hours. The Italian bread is usually made either as a round or as an oblong loaf with pointed ends. This type of make-up yields larger slices and makes this bread suitable for sandwiches. The make-up of Vienna bread is usually in the oblong shape.

After proofing and prior to baking, all three types of bread are cut in the top crust to prevent formation of wild breaks during the early phase of baking. French bread is cut four times diagonally across the loaf. These cuts usually overlap by about one third of their length. The heavy steam used during the first minutes of baking tends to keep the crust soft during the expansion (*oven kick*) period and will allow the wide expansion of the cuts.

The round Italian loaves receive two parallel cuts in one direction and two more parallel cuts across the first two cuts. The oblong Italian loaves are either cut three or four times straight across, or once lengthwise and slightly off-center. These long cuts will generally open wide during baking. There are also many other methods a baker of Italian bread can use to make his breads look attractive. In contrast to French bread, Italian bread is baked without steam for a thick, dull crust. This heavy crust contributes to the good taste of this bread.

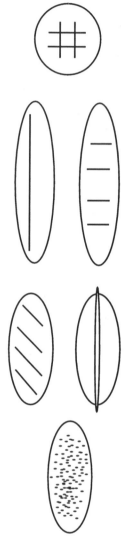

The Vienna bread is usually formed into an oblong shape. The almost fully proofed loaves are either cut three or four times diagonally across the top, or they are topped with a thin moist dough strip placed lengthwise across the loaf. This dough strip will cause the loaf to form a wide break along one of its sides. Vienna bread may also be topped with poppy or sesame seed, or covered with a *Dutch Crunch Topping*. Topped breads are not cut prior to baking. For best appearance, Vienna bread is baked, like French bread, with a good amount of low pressure steam. This will assure that the bread has a crispy crust with a nice sheen, or bloom.

Although the sponge and dough method tends to produce bread of a slightly better overall quality, good quality breads can also be produced by the straight dough method.

When these breads are baked directly on the oven hearth, the moulded dough pieces are generally placed and proofed on peel boards covered with a thin layer of coarse corn meal, or on perforated and glazed metal trays. Some bakers also use, with good results, sheet pans lined with treated paper or a non-stick Teflon® fabric, trays and pans eliminate the transfer of the proofed dough pieces to the oven hearth and facilitate the removal of the bread from the oven. However, the residual corn meal in the bottom crust of bread loaded into the oven with a peel board contributes to the good taste of the bottom bread crust.

Since the eating quality of bread baked directly on the oven hearth depends on the crispness of the bread crust, these breads have a relatively short shelf-life. Moisture migrating from the crumb to the crust softens and toughens the crust when the bread is protected from drying out, i.e., when it is packaged in polyethylene bags. In order to slow down the drying out of this product and to keep its crust in a crisp state, this bread is best stored and sold in waxed paper or in perforated plastic bags.

Formula 18
French Bread
(Sponge and Dough Method

Baker's Percent	Weight lb.	oz.	Ingredients
			Sponge: (Preferment)
64	4	0	Bread Flour (Spring Patent)
0.5		0.5	Mineral Yeast Food
2.5		2.5	Compressed Yeast
37.5	2	5.5	Water
			Dough: (Remix)
36	2	4	Bread Flour (Spring Patent)
1.5		1.5	42% High-Fructose Corn Syrup (71% Solids)
1.75		1.75	Salt
1		1	Non-Diastatic Dry Malt
1		1	Bread Shortening
1		1	Compressed Yeast
18	1	2	Water and Ice
164.75	**10**	**4.75**	**Total Amount**

Sponge: *Temperature:* 74-77°F (24-25°C).
Fermentation Time: 3.5-4 hours at 84°F (29°C).

Dough: *Mix:* To full gluten development.
Temperature: 78-80°F (25.5-26.5°C).
Floor Time: 15 minutes under ambient conditions.

Scaling Weight: 14 ounces (400 grams) dough per 12 ounce (340 grams) loaf.

Intermediate Proof: 15 to 20 minutes under ambient conditions.

Mould: Form long loaves approximately 22 inches (55 centimeters) long and place loaves on peel boards dusted with corn meal or on glazed perforated metal baking trays.

Proof: Approximately one hour at 104°F (40°C) with 80% relative humidity (not quite full proof).

Cutting: Four long cuts diagonally across loaf (overlapping by one third of the length of the cuts).

Bake: Approximately 25 minutes at 430°F (221°C) with heavy low-pressure steam for the first five minutes of baking time.

Formula 19
Italian Bread
(Straight Dough Method)

Baker's Percent	Weight lb.	oz.	Ingredients
100	6	4	Bread Flour (Spring Patent)
3		3	Granulated Sugar
2		2	Salt
1		1	Bread Shortening
0.25		0.25	Ethoxylated Monoglycerides
2.5		2.5	Compressed Yeast
0.006		(60 ppm)	Ascorbic Acid
59	3	11	Water and Ice
167.756	**10**	**7.75**	**Total Amount**

Dough: *Mix:* To full gluten development.
Temperature: 80°F (26.5°C).
Floor Time: 10 minutes under ambient conditions.

Scaling Weight: 23 ounces (650 grams) dough per 1 1/4 pound (567 gram) loaf.

Intermediate Proof: 15 to 20 minutes under ambient conditions.

Mould: Form loaves into desired shape: round or oblong with pointed ends for baking directly on oven hearth or perforated metal tray. Place shaped loaves on wooden peels covered with a thin layer of corn meal for easy transfer to the oven hearth. Loaves may also be baked in glazed perforated metal basket pans used for baking rye breads.

Proof: 60 to 65 minutes at 104°F (40°C) and 80% relative humidity to slightly less than full proof.

Cutting: Cut oblong loaves once lengthwise or three to four times across. Cut round loaves twice in one direction and twice across the first two parallel cuts.

Bake: 28 to 30 minutes at 430°F (221°C). For best flavor, this bread should have a thick and heavy crust. However, when a thinner and a shiny crust is preferred, use heavy steam during the first five minutes baking time.

Formula 20
Vienna Bread
(Sponge and Dough Method)

Baker's Percent	Weight lb.	oz.	Ingredients
			Sponge: (Preferment)
64	4	0	Bread Flour (Spring Patent)
0.5		0.5	Mineral Yeast Food
2.5		2.5	Compressed Yeast
38	2	6	Water
			Dough: (Remix)
33.5	2	1.5	Bread Flour (Spring Patent)
2.5		2.5	Potato Flour
2.5		2.5	Nonfat Dry Milk or Replacer
1		1	Dried Whole Eggs
2.2		2.2	Salt
2		2	Bread Shortening
20	1	4	Water and Ice
168.7	**10**	**8.7**	**Total Amount**

Sponge: *Temperature:* 75-77°F (24-25°C).
Fermentation Time: 3.5-4 hours at 84°F (29°C).

Dough: *Mix*: To full gluten development.
Temperature: 78-80°F (25.5-26.5°C).
Floor Time: 10 to 15 minutes under ambient conditions.

Scaling Weight: 23 ounces (650 grams) dough per 1 1/4 pound (567 gram) loaf.

Intermediate Proof: 10 to 15 minutes under ambient conditions.

Mould: Form dough pieces into oblong loaves with pointed ends for baking directly on the oven hearth or on a glazed perforated metal tray. Shape dough with blunt ends for baking in glazed perforated metal basket pans. Loaves to be baked directly on the oven hearth are placed on wooden peels covered with a thin layer of corn meal for easy transfer to the oven hearth.

Proof: 60 to 65 minutes at 104°F (40°C) and 80% relative humidity to slightly less than full proof.

Topping

Plain: Place a thin moist strip of dough over the full length of the loaf and tuck ends of strip under the ends of the loaf. These loaves may be egg-washed.

Seeds: Spray top surface of loaves with water and sprinkle 0.5 ounce sesame or poppy seed on top of the loaves. Cut loaves once across their full length.

Dutch Crust Topping: After moulding and before panning and proofing, dip top of dough pieces into the special topping (1.5 to 2 ounces topping per loaf). These loaves are not cut before baking!

Bake: 28 to 30 minutes at 430°F (221°C) with heavy low pressure (wet) steam during the first five minutes of baking.

Formula 21
Dutch Crust Topping

True Percent	Weight lb.	oz.	Ingredients
	1) Combine to form a paste:		
39.6	10	0	Rice Flour
4	1	0	Granulated Sugar
1		4	Salt
4	1	0	Compressed Yeast
31.6	8	0	Water
	2) Hot slurry added to above:		
15.8	4	0	Hot Water (170°F or 77°C)
4	1	0	Margarine (melted in hot water)
100	**25**	**4**	**Total Amount**

Mix: To a smooth soft paste free of lumps.

Floor Time: One hour under ambient conditions.

Rye Breads

Rye breads are very popular in central and east Europe. While practically all of the rye bread in Europe is still baked directly on the oven hearth, much of the rye bread produced by large wholesale bakeries on the North American continent is baked in glazed perforated metal basket pans. These basket pans are usually strapped together in multiple units and enable the bakery to produce rye breads with the same equipment used for other pan breads.

Although bread can be made from 100% rye flour, most of the rye bread is made from primarily wheat flour and not more than 40% rye flour in the total flour blend. As a general rule, the more rye flour and the darker the rye flour (containing more bran), the smaller the volume of the resulting bread. The protein in rye flour does not form gluten during mixing and the structure of rye bread depends on the protein added with the wheat flour.

Another factor in the volume of rye bread is the amount of sugar added to the dough. By starving the yeast (withholding fermentable sugar) during the early stages of baking, expansion of the loaves in the oven is restricted and a denser product is obtained. Slightly higher levels of salt are also used for this purpose. Limiting the expansion of rye bread often becomes necessary to prevent the "bursting" of loaves during baking.

Usually, the more expanded rye breads are baked in perforated basket pans and the heavier breads are baked either directly on the oven hearth or on perforated metal trays.

In order to produce a well leavened bread, rye flours are generally used in combination with a very strong wheat flour. In the past, this flour was usually a *first clear flour*, a flour fraction separated from the *patent flour* during the milling process. This flour is also know as *fancy clear flour.* However, because of changes in flour specifications, "fancy clear flour" is no longer readily available and many bakers have replaced this flour with a *high gluten flour*.

Since the non-gluten forming rye flour reduces the dough strength, loaves made from doughs formulated with more than 20% rye flour are usually cut across the top and are baked with plenty of low pressure steam to prevent wild breaks or bursting. Since rye breads made from more than 40% rye flour usually do not expand very much during baking, they are *docked* rather than cut. The process of "docking" consists of punching holes into the proofed product with a sharp pointed object, like a large nail or a thin sharpened dowel rod.

All breads made with a significant amount of rye flour (more than 25% f.b.) benefit from a high volume of low pressure steam during the first five minutes of baking. The steam helps to prevent wild breaks in the bread crust and will give the crust a glossy appearance. Bakers who do not have steam available in their ovens brush the hot loaves right after their removal from the oven either with a melted margarine or with a starch wash made from one part corn starch and 15-20 parts of water. Regular corn starch must be gelatinized by cooking until it "turns clear." Pregelatinized starch may also be used, but it is more difficult to prepare a lump-free slurry with pregelatinized starch.

Formula 22
Jewish Rye Bread
(Straight Dough Method)

Baker's Percent	Weight lb.	oz.	Ingredients
40	2	8	Light Rye Flour
60	3	12	Clear Flour
2		2	Vital Wheat Gluten
2		2	White Sour
1		1	42% High-Fructose Corn Syrup (71% Solids)
2.2		2.2	Salt
0.5		0.5	Ethoxylated Monoglycerides
2		2	Bread Shortening
2.5		2.5	Compressed Yeast
0.012	(120 ppm)		Ascorbic Acid
63	3	15	Water
Soaked Caraway Seed (3 hours)			
1.5		1.5	Whole Caraway Seed
1.5		1.5	Water (86°F or 30°C)
178.212	11	2.2	Total Amount

Dough: *Mix:* Until dough is smooth and developed.
Temperature: 80°F (26.5°C).
Floor Time: 5 minutes under ambient conditions.

Scaling Weight: 27 ounces (766 grams) dough per 1 1/2 pound (680 gram) loaf.

Intermediate Proof: 15 to 20 minutes under ambient conditions.

Mould: Form round or oblong loaves as desired and place moulded loaves on peel boards covered with a thin layer of cornmeal. Dough pieces may also be placed in reed baskets for proofing. After proofing, baskets are turned over onto corn-mealed peel boards for baking directly on the oven hearth.

Proof: 60-65 minutes at 104°F (40°C) with 80% relative humidity.

Cutting: Cut round loaves twice across the loaf and twice across the first two cuts. Cut oblong loaves three times across the top.

Bake: 30 to 35 minutes at 430°F (221°C) with high volume steam during the first five minutes of bake.
Note: To improve the appearance of the bread, brush with gelatinized starch wash immediately after baking.

Formula 23
Delicatessen Rye
(Sponge and Dough Method)

Baker's Percent	Weight lb.	oz.	Ingredients
			Sponge: (Preferment)
32	2	0	Bread Flour
8		8	Dark Rye Flour
20	1	4	Light Rye Flour
4		4	Rye Sour
0.5		0.5	Mineral Yeast Food
2		2	Whole Caraway Seed
0.1		0.1	Dry Caramel Color
1.5		1.5	Compressed Yeast
37	2	5	Water
			Dough: (Remix)
40	2	8	Clear Flour
4.5		4.5	42% High-Fructose Corn Syrup (71% Solids)
2.25		2.25	Salt
0.25		0.25	Rye Bread Flavor
1.5		1.5	Bread Shortening
0.5		0.5	Crumb Softener
21.5	1	5.5	Water and Ice
175.6	**10**	**15.6**	**Total Amount**

Sponge: *Temperature:* 74°F (23.5°C).
Fermentation Time: 3.5 to 4 hours at 84°F (29°C).

Dough: *Mix:* Until dough is smooth. Do not overmix!
Temperature: 76°F (24.5°C).
Floor Time: 15 minutes.

Scaling Weight: 36 ounces (1020 grams) dough per 2 pound (908 gram) loaf.

Mould: Form dough pieces into 15 inch (38 centimeter) long loaves and place in glazed perforated metal basket pan

Proof: 60-65 minutes at 104°F (40°C) with 80% relative humidity. After proofing, dock each loaf seven times and two inches (5 centimeter) deep

Bake: 30 minutes at 400°F (205°C) with high volume steam during the first five minutes

Cool: One hour under ambient conditions on rack or conveyor
Note: These loaves may be sliced and divided into two one pound (454 gram) loaves

Formula 24
German Pumpernickel
(Sponge and Dough Method)

Baker's Percent	Weight lb.	oz.	Ingredients
			Sponge: (Preferment)
30	1	14	Clear Flour
12.5		12.5	Medium Pumpernickel Meal
7.5		7.5	Dark Rye Flour
15		15	Light Rye Flour
4		4	Rye Sour
0.5		0.5	Mineral Yeast Food
0.3		0.3	Ground Caraway Seed
1.5		1.5	Dry Caramel Color
1.5		1.5	Compressed Yeast
40	2	8	Water
			Dough: (Remix)
32.5	2	0.5	Clear Flour
2.5		2.5	Vital Wheat Gluten
4.5		4.5	42% High-Fructose Corn Syrup (71% Solids)
2.1		2.1	Salt
0.3		0.3	Rye Bread Flavor
1.5		1.5	Bread Shortening
0.2		0.2	Compressed Yeast
24	1	8	Water and Ice
180.4	**11**	**4.4**	**Total Amount**

Sponge: *Temperature:* 75°F (24°C).
Fermentation Time: 3.5-4 hours at 84°F (29°C).

Dough: *Mix:* Until Dough is smooth. Do not overmix!
Temperature: 78°F (25.5°C).
Floor Time: 15 minutes under ambient conditions.

Scaling Weight: 19 ounces (540 grams) of dough per 1 pound (454 gram) loaf.

Mould: Shape loaves into round loaves and dip into coarse pumpernickel meal for topping.
Note: These loaves may be baked directly on the oven hearth, on a pie plate, or in a shallow round pan.

Proof 60-65 minutes at 104°F (40°C) with 80% relative humidity. After proofing, dock loaves five times 2 inches (5 centimeters) deep with a docking tool.

Bake: 28-30 minutes at 400°F (205°C) with steam for the first five minutes baking time.

Cool: One hour under ambient conditions on rack or conveyor.

Formula 25
Milwaukee Sour Rye
(Sponge and Dough Method)

Baker's Percent	Weight lb.	oz.	Ingredients
			Sponge: (Preferment)
38	2	6	Clear Flour
20	1	4	Dark Rye Flour
2		2	Vital Wheat Gluten
4.5		4.5	Rye Sour
0.5		0.5	Mineral Yeast Food
0.5		0.5	Salt
0.8		0.8	Whole Caraway Seed
0.15		0.15	Dry Caramel Color
1.75		1.75	Compressed Yeast
40	2	8	Water
			Dough: (Remix)
40	2	8	Clear Flour
1		1	Granulated Sugar
1.5		1.5	Salt
0.3		0.3	Rye Bread Flavor
1.5		1.5	Bread Shortening
27	1	11	Water and Ice
179.5	**11**	**3.5**	**Total Amount**

Sponge: *Temperature:* 75°F (24°C).
Fermentation Time: 3.5-4 hours at 84°F (29°C).

Dough: *Mix:* To full gluten development; but do not overmix!
Temperature: 77°F (25°C).
Floor Time: 15 minutes.

Scaling Weight: 19 ounces (540 grams) dough per 1 pound (454 gram) loaf.

Mould: Loaves to be baked in 9 3/4 inch (25 centimeter) long perforated basket pans.

Proof: 60 to 65 minutes at 109°F (43°C) with 80% relative humidity.

Bake: 20 to 22 minutes at 420°F (215°C) with high volume steam during first five minutes of baking.

Cool: One hour under ambient conditions on rack or conveyor.

Formula 26
Swedish Dark Rye
(Sponge and Dough Method)

Baker's Percent	Weight lb.	oz.	Ingredients
			Sponge: (Preferment)
15	15		Dark Rye Flour
0.1		0.1	Ground Anise Seed
2		2	Compressed Yeast
30	1	14	Water
			Dough: (Remix)
85	5	5	Clear Flour
3		3	Vital Wheat Gluten
8		8	Liquid Molasses
2.25		2.25	Salt
0.1		0.1	Ground Cardamon
2		2	Orange Peel
0.25		0.25	Ethoxylated Monoglycerides
4		4	Bread Shortening
25	1	9	Water and Ice
			Soaked Raisins: (1 hour)
10		10	Raisins
2.5		2.5	Water
189.2	**11**	**13.2**	**Total Amount**

Sponge: *Temperature:* 76°F (24.5°C).
Fermentation Time: 3.5-4 hours at 84°F (29°C).

Dough: *Mix:* To slightly less than full gluten development before incorporating the soaked raisins. Do not overmix!
Temperature: 80°F (26.5°C).
Floor Time: 25 minutes under ambient conditions.

Scaling Weight: 23 ounces (650 grams) dough per 1 1/4 pound (568 gram) loaf.

Mould: Shape round loaves and place them in 8 inch (20 cm) round or square pans.

Proof: 60 to 65 minutes to full proof at 104°F (40°C) with 80% relative humidity.

Cutting: Although this bread does not need to be cut, some bakers cut a small cross into the top crust, strictly for a decorative purpose.

Bake: 35 minutes at 430°F (221°C) without steam.
Note: To improve the eye appeal of the bread, brush the loaves with a starch wash immediately after removal from the oven.

Corn Bread

White pan bread containing a significant amount of corn meal was very popular in the United States during the first half of the 20th century. It lost its appeal to the consumer when the baking industry emphasized the softness and moistness (freshness) of bread. However, corn meal used at a moderate level can transform an ordinary white pan bread to a delicious variety product.

Since yellow dent corn has a distinct taste not appreciated by many consumers when it is very intense, it is recommended to use corn meal for replacing flour in corn pan bread. In contrast to corn flour, corn meal has a milder corn taste and it also contributes to the texture of the baked product. Coarse corn meal gives a "crunchy" bite, while corn flour does not affect the mouthfeel of the product significantly, but contributes a very strong taste.

Formula 27
Corn Bread with Raisins
(Sponge and Dough Method)

Baker's Percent	Weight lb.	oz.	Ingredients
			Sponge: (Preferment)
55	3	7	Bread Flour (Spring Patent)
15		15	Yellow Corn Meal
0.5		0.5	Mineral Yeast Food
2.5		2.5	Compressed Yeast
42	2	10	Water
			Dough: (Remix)
30	1	14	Bread Flour (Spring Patent)
8		8	Brown Sugar
2		2	Nonfat Dry Milk or Replacer
2		2	Salt
3		3	Bread Shortening
18	1	2	Water and Ice
			Soaked Raisins: (1 hour)
16	1	0	Raisins
4		4	Water
198	12	6	**Total Amount**

Sponge: *Temperature:* 74-77°F (23.5-25°C).
Fermentation Time: 3.5-4 hours at 84°F (29°C).

Dough: *Mix:* To full gluten development before incorporation of soaked raisins.
Temperature: 78-80°F (25.5-26.5°C).
Floor Time: 10 to 15 min. under ambient conditions.

Scaling Weight: 18.5 ounces (525 grams) dough per 1 pound (454 gram) loaf.

Proof: 60-65 minutes at 109°F (43°C) to full proof.

Bake: 16-18 minutes at 450°F (232°C).

Cool: One hour under ambient conditions on rack or conveyor.

References

Lahvic, R., *Industry Business*, Bakery, February 1991 (17)

Lahvic, R. and Malovanic, D., *Wholesale Trends '92*, Bakery Production and Marketing, June 1992 (60)

Anonymous, *Flaxseed Bulletin*, Omega Research Series, February 1994

Index

high fiber pan bread 216
high gluten flour 225
high-fiber bread 125, 214
high-fructose corn syrup 12, 112,
    113, 114
high-intensity sweeteners 120
honey 118, 119, 120
honey bran bread 198, 200
humidity 182
hydration 165
hydrolysis 113
hydroperoxide 150
hypertension 105

I

imported molasses 117
infrared radiation heat 51
ingredient specification 67,
    68, 71, 185
insoluble fiber 125
instant dry yeast 100
intermediate proofing 174
invert sugar 118
invertase 109
iodates 83
iodized salt 104
iron 81, 82
iron filings 161
isomerase 114
Italian bread 216, 218, 221

J

Jewish rye bread 226

K

keyhole effect 129

L

L-cysteine 7, 147, 148, 170
lactic acid bacteria 13, 96
lactose 107, 108
lard 121
lecithin 124
levulose 107
light" or "lite 125
light sour 15
lipoxygenase 150
liquid sponges 9, 10
low calorie 125

M

macadamia nuts 137
Maillard reaction 109, 112, 116,
    123
malt extract 164
malt syrups 116
malted flour 149
maltose 107, 114, 115
maturing agent 7, 87
McDuffee bowl 77
medium rye flour 92
microbial spoilage 156
microorganisms 13
milk bread 123
milk replacers 123, 187
milk solids 187
mill feed 88
mill molasses 117
milled flaxseed 202
millet 201
milling techniques 65
Milwaukee sour rye 229
mineral yeast food 94, 141
minerals 119
Mixatron 166

mixer, high-speed BiPlex 22
mixer, Tweedy 22
mixer, double arm 22
mixer, horizontal 22
mixer, spiral 22
Mixograph 72, 73
modified atmosphere packaging
    161, 162
molasses 117, 202
mold 55, 57, 156, 160
monocalcium phosphate
    7, 94, 141
monoglyceride 122, 153, 155
monosaccharides 107
multi-grain 93
multi-grain blends 203
multi-grain bread 90, 201, 202,
    204
muscat raisins 134

N

natural preservative 133, 136, 160
nitrogen trichloride 83
no-time straight dough 6, 7, 97,
    147, 170, 185
non-diastatic malt 115, 116
non-wheat grains 92
nonfat dry milk 122, 123
nutmeats 137

O

oat 201, 202
oat bran 129
oat fiber 129
oat flakes 208
oatmeal bread 208
onion 138, 140
organic acids
    13, 14, 95, 96, 136, 160, 178

oven, deck 49
oven, designs 51
oven, reel 47
oven spring 136
oven, traveling tray 47, 52
oven, tunnel 47, 52
ovens, direct fired 46, 47
ovens, indirectly fired 46
overbaking 181
overhead proofer 35, 174
oxidizing agents 83, 142, 143, 147
oxygen 161

P

papain 150
patent flour 88, 89
peanuts 137
pecans 137
pentosans 125
perforated plastic bags 219
pesticides 71
pin mixers 28
plastic sponges 8, 9, 10
pocket dividers 29
polysaccharides 108
polysorbate 60 151
poppy seeds 138, 201, 208
potassium bromate
    83, 142, 143, 146, 165, 170
potassium chloride 105
potassium iodate 145
potassium sorbate 158
preferment 8, 142, 150, 153,
    168, 170, 178, 185, 195, 215
preservative 56, 156, 157, 183
press dividers 33
pressure board 176
processing aid 143
product loaders 54
product unloaders 54
proof box 178

straight grade flour 88
straight grain moulder 37
substrate 14
succinylated monoglycerides 151
sucrose 107, 108, 109, 110, 111
sugar 107, 108
sugar spots 112
sulfhydryl groups 143
sulfur dioxide 118, 134
sunflower seed kernels 201
surfactants 151
Swedish dark rye 230
sweet doughs 97
Swiss peasant bread 213

T

tartaric acid 160
temperature of preferments 9
tendercurl moulder 38
topping seeds 138, 139
toxins 71
tricalcium phosphate 106
triticale 201
tyers 60

V

vegetable oil 187
Vienna bread 216, 218, 222
vinegar 159
vital wheat gluten 214
vitamins 81, 119

W

water 93
water activity
    118, 133, 135, 162, 183
water brews 11, 12

waterjets 54
wheat bran 125, 202
wheat bread 194, 195
wheat germ 88, 194
wheat gluten 20, 63, 90, 128,
    130, 131, 195, 201, 203
wheat 'n' rye bread 210
Wheat Quality Council 65
whey 123
white flour 87
white pan bread 187, 188,
    190, 191, 192, 193
white rye flour 92
whole wheat 89, 211
whole wheat bread 90, 120, 132,
    194, 196, 197
whole wheat flour 194, 210
wild breaks 217, 225
wild yeast 56, 178
wrapping machines 58

X

xanthophyll 86

Y

yeast 4, 9, 94, 95, 96, 114, 136,
142, 157, 159, 160, 164, 165,
171, 178, 224
yellow prussiate of soda 104

Z

zante currants 134
zymase enzyme system 109